WALKING INTO YOUR PROMISE

EBONY BUTLER

WESTBOW
PRESS®
A DIVISION OF THOMAS NELSON
& ZONDERVAN

WestBow Press books may be ordered through booksellers or by contacting:

WestBow Press
A Division of Thomas Nelson & Zondervan
1663 Liberty Drive
Bloomington, IN 47403
www.westbowpress.com
844-714-3454

ISBN: 978-1-6642-9863-7 (sc)
ISBN: 978-1-6642-9864-4 (e)

Library of Congress Control Number: 2023908061

Print information available on the last page.

WestBow Press rev. date: 05/15/2023

Contents

Dedication

Have you ever been in a season, where God has revealed to you his promises for your life, but you have not successfully reached it yet? God has revealed to you wealth, marriage, newness, children, prosperity, but no matter how much you give God your all in hopes to receive his promises, you are still waiting.

Or instead, you have some of the following things listed above from God, but what God has promised you was peace, strength, mercy, love, grace, and hope. However, you still find yourself feeling depressed, stressed, worrying, weak and tired.

Whether you feel either way, then this book is dedicated to you! Allow this book to give you access to tools and resources needed to unlock your promise in the kingdom and inherit it here, on earth.

If you are one who does not feel either way and feels as if you are waiting for God to reveal his promises to you, then this book is also dedicated to you. This book will help you to see and hear from God more clearly. God is always speaking, it is up to us to listen.

Maybe, you have already received your promise from God. Do not think this book is not dedicated to you, because it is! God ALWAYS has more in store for us! God's promises are never ending! Allow God to speak to you and through you so you can unlock more promises from God.

Lastly, you may feel as though you simply do not need any promises from God. Please always aim to use wisdom to understand we all need promises from God, in order to build our relationship with him. If you fit in this category, this book is most importantly dedicated to you. Start your journey building a relationship with God and he will change you for the better.

As you can see, this book is dedicated to each and every reader that reads this book! I pray God's favor and blessings upon every one of your lives!

Remember the best is yet to come! While you wait for the best to happen, walk with God and allow God to direct your path. Your path with God will ultimately lead you into your promise.

Preface

It is easier to get upset with God when things do not go our way versus understanding God's process. God's process may sometimes seem to not make sense. However God never intended for us to understand why things happen the way they do. God only wants us to trust his process in order to understand—in time. *Proverbs verse 3:5-6* tells us to, *Trust in the Lord with all your heart: do not depend on your own understanding. Seek his will in all you do, and he will show you which path to take.*

Do not stray away from God or your path will be much longer and harder. Failure to be obedient to trusting God's process results in us having to wait longer than what God intended us to, to obtain his promises. Obedience is ALWAYS better than sacrifice.

This story started as a diary from a traumatic break up between someone God told me would become my husband and lifetime partner. This heart break was so detrimental because this man was my best friend before our relationship.

In the beginning of my diary, I discussed each day, how I was so wrapped up into my emotions. Although my feelings were trying to consume me into depression, I tried to see God in everything. The word of God tells me that all paths will lead back to God. I was not realizing that God was using my break up to remind me of his promise he said to me. God gave me my promise before I entered my mother's womb. For the Lord said in Jeremiah 5 verse 1, *I knew you before I formed you in your mother's womb.*

I had no idea that my promise would ultimately catch my attention throughout my break up process with my significant other, but all things work together for the good of those that love the Lord.

Here I was, blaming the devil for the mess in my life, when God created the mess, to grab my attention. The only thing the devil wanted was for me to forfeit my promise, again, but it was this time that I fought. In the end, I won! You want to know why? See God has always promised me that I would become an author, since I was a child. However my gift of writing was always overlooked because I was not passionate about it.

Growing up, I received A's on every one of my papers in school and in college. My essays were written so well that I made the dean's list.

One night after giving birth to my son, God told me to write my book. Lord knows when I had my son, I went through the worst experiences with my child's father. So, I knew my story needed to be heard, but I do not believe I was ready to tell it back then.

After that night, I went to church and the pastor asked me to come up to the altar for prayer. He said to me, "Ebony God said write your book. You have the creativity and the knowledge to reach others. Do not underestimate yourself. God is going to bless you more than you can imagine, when you write this book."

Years before this pastor had given me this word from God, a prophet told me that I would be blessed from telling others my story. I had no idea what that meant because I was only a child. My bishop at my home church even told me when I was fourteen, that I would grow up preaching God's word. He prayed for me and said, "This girl is going to be preaching!"

Recently, before I wrote this book, a pastor, once again, made me come up to the front altar for prayer. He said, "Ebony, you are going to be preaching! You are going to change people's lives!" The pastor also said, "Make sure someone calls me when she preaches her first sermon, because I will make sure I will be there!" In my mind I was like, "Yeah, ok. Preach what? That is not happening at all!"

A few weeks after this pastor spoke this word over my life, my mom called me, who is also my pastor, and said "God showed me he was birthing ministry in you. You will be preaching and taking after me." I responded to her, "I have no idea what everyone is seeing from God and why God did not show me that. If God did not show me that, it is not going to happen. Not in this lifetime!"

You see how everything that happens in your life will always lead back to God's divine purpose for your life? Although God promised me to become an author and the many blessings that I will receive once I became one, God's purpose was ultimately for me to spread his word.

Your promise will never be a one and done situation. When God opens the door to your promise, you will enter a room that will have multiple doors inside of it. Entering the door to our promise leads to doors that open up our purpose, our assignments, our gifts, and most importantly our blessings.

So, when I fought throughout this breakup, which was the fight between trusting God's plan and wanting my plan, I did not realize what I had won. I unlocked doors accessing my purpose, my assignments, my gifts, and my rewards. The fight was one of the most challenging battles I could ever fight through, but I still won and I have the victory in Jesus! How did I know that I won? It is because you are holding my promise in your hand, which is this book.

Regardless if my message reaches your heart or not, I did what God instructed me to do. You are the reason I have one of the blessings that God promised me! Simply because you purchased my book. So, I thank you!

Remember to always trust God's will, so that it can lead you into your promise!

Acknowledgement

First and foremost, I would like to give honor and reverence to my Lord and savior, Jesus Christ. I am thankful that God has graced me with his wisdom and knowledge to be able to share my testimony with others. I am forever grateful and blessed to serve an awesome, mighty God! God allowed me to write this book and God used me through writing this book to save the lives of many! I pray this book impacts the lives of all those who read it, in a miraculous way! Thank you, heavenly father, for everything you have done for me! I am because of you!

Secondly, I would like to thank my life partner, my soul mate, and my best friend, Gary Brown. Had I never met Gary, this story could not be written. Thank you, Gary, for never giving up on us. Thank you, Gary, for loving me in God's image. I thank God for allowing us to connect physically and spiritually. God knew I needed you. I love you now and forever more.

To my dearest son, Quron Yuille Jr., you are my heart. I love you more than life itself. Thank you for always being one of mommy's biggest supporters. Quron, you are the most loving, kindest, athletic, and intelligent kid I know! You changed my life the moment God created you in my womb. Had I never had you, my life would be incomplete and this book could not exist. Thank you, son, for being the person to help me grow! You are my greatest blessing from God!

Mom, you are the most influential person on this planet. You are the epitome of what a Godly woman represents. I would not be who I am today, without everything you have instilled into me. I honor you in every way! Thank you for teaching me how to be graceful, how to put God first in my life, giving me wisdom, nurturing me with your love and being my biggest cheerleader! Mom, you are truly my best friend! I love you always!

To my stepmom, Shinelle, thank you for always pushing me! You believed in me on days I did not believe in myself. You taught me that excellence was my ONLY option in life. I truly believe had I not had you rooting for me consistently, I would have not accomplished writing this book. You have inspired me in so many ways to rise above every circumstance. So, I thank you for being a great second mom to me!

To conclude, I would like to thank everyone reading this book. I believe everyone who reads, will gain God's strength and wisdom to have the ability to access their promise! Thank you! Thank you! Thank you!

Introduction

2 Peter 1:3-5 | NIV

3 By his divine power, God has given us everything we need for living a godly life. We have received all of this by coming to know him, the one who called us to himself by means of his marvelous glory and excellence. 4 And because of his glory and excellence, he has given us great and precious promises. These are promises that enable you to share his divine nature and escape the world's corruption caused by human desires. 5 In view of all of this, make every effort to respond to God's promises.

2 Peter 3:9 | NIV

9 The Lord isn't really being slow about his promise, as some people think. No, he is being patient for your sake. He does not want anyone to be destroyed, but wants everyone to repent.

It is time for you to walk into your promise and access everything God has in store for you. Although you may have been waiting for your promise your entire life, understand God has not forgotten! If he is making you wait, it is because he is waiting for something from you! Use this reading as a guide to remember God has great things ahead of you! You can only reach those things when you align your path with his will!

Chapter 1

THE ASSIGNMENT

DAY 1

Today was ruff.

I barely could get out of bed.

I went into the bathroom and told God at approximately five o' clock am, that I was upset with him. Why am I always the one getting hurt? Why can I not just be happy with someone? I did not even ask for a relationship or think to look for one, it came to me, literally, and I fell for him hard.

My heart could not bear being away from the man I love, adore and cherish.

I started to become emotional.

While taking my frustrations out to God in prayer, my son bombarded me in the bathroom, opening the door and asking me to go back to bed. I rushed to wipe my tears off and pretended I was on my phone. I told my son I'll be in bed soon, although honestly, I did not want to go to bed with a broken heart. I guess all I wanted was a quick "I love you text".

Although the breakup process can be ruff, reassurance of the love we shared can help to mend my broken heart.

I tried to pretend as if my emotions did not exist when my son interrupted my crying session. I did not want my son worrying about me, so I went back to sleep with him.

I woke up again at ten o' clock am and sat on my couch in my living room. I began to kneel on my knees and pray, asking God to give me strength. I continued by asking God to bring Gerald and I together sooner than ninety days.

After praying, I laid down until twelve o' clock pm, took a relaxing shower and prayed again. This time my prayer was altered. I told God thank you! With a mouth full of thanksgiving and a heart full of praise I told God, I will bless his name at all times.

My worship really moved me in a tremendous way, that I began crying, thankful tears this time. Tears of gratitude. Despite how I feel or what I may be going through God has kept me and has been faithful to me. Sitting in God's presence, there truly is fullness of joy!

After praising God in the shower, I went into my room to get dressed.

As I sat on my bed, throwing my hoodie on, God revealed to me my assignment. The assignment was to fast for fifth teen days, and January 1, 2023, Gerald will be back.

This time when Gerald returns the relationship will be better than ever.

God spoke to me, once more, and instructed me to be specific when praying for Gerald's return home. God said to me, "Gerald is under attack and needs to leave the place he is residing at". I was worried when God told me that, but I knew I had to be obedient when God speaks.

So, I am attempting to do this for Gerald. I will commit to completing this fast. This is not just for Gerald, but for us both. I am going to remember what God told me before this all happened.

Furthermore, my self love-fast will continue, however I have to trust God on a new level. A higher level. A level I have not reached yet.

God is not a man he should lie, if he said it, it will come to pass. So, I believe that on January the 1st of the year 2023, Gerald and I will be back together again and we will stay together this time; inseparable.

Sincerely,
A firm believer.

Chapter 2

GOD'S MESSENGERS

DAY 2

Dear Diary,   *December 17, 2022*

Today started off amazing.

The day began peacefully.

Although at midnight, I had to pray harder than I did last night. I began to feel something happening in the spirit realm, something unexplainable.

However, back to earlier today, I woke up smiling and I prayed.

Afterwards, I went into the shower and I worshiped God. My praises turned into tears of joy, rejoicing before the Lord. Here I am, feeling miserable on the inside, but God's peace will truly surpass our understanding.

Once I had finished showering, I put my clothes on, danced around the house and made breakfast. I proceeded to spend quality time with my son and prepared for my mom's house warming event.

As I sat in front of my vanity mirror, putting my makeup on, I received some missed calls from my friend. It had to be important because my friend does not call me back to back often.

When I looked at my call history on my phone, I even noticed that she called me twice at seven o' clock this morning as well. So now, I am nervous. I called her back and when she answered she said, "Gerald called me last night on FaceTime, stating he had a lot to drink, coming from a party." Gerald continued on, telling her he is still in love with me and wished things did not have to be this way. He did not want the information to get back to me, so he told her to keep this secret. Then, Gerald goes on to even address the fight we were in, saying, "Could you honestly take back a person who can be so manipulative?" My friend replied, "Gerald, I thought you both moved past this argument?" Gerald states, "Yeah, but I'm still hurt."

My friend told Gerald that she could not voice her opinion because she is my friend first, so she cannot pick a side and ended the phone call.

Now I know you're wondering, why does Gerald have my friend's phone number? Gerald's friends and my friends are our family. We both have all of our friends' phone numbers. So that we can communicate if and when we need to. It is not to ever be messy, but because of how deep we value and love our friends.

I truly respected my friend hanging up and not voicing her opinion, but most importantly communicating to me what had happened. I can not lie though, it was still very hurtful. Hurtful on Gerald's side of course and inconsiderate for Gerald to call my friend late at night, while being intoxicated. Here I am praying, fasting, believing God for Gerald and he's not thinking things through. Gerald was probably at that party getting other females' phone numbers and still drinking his pain away. Honestly, I feel lost. Why is it that I am holding on to a person that can make me appear so foolish? If the roles became reversed, he would be upset.

Now with my makeup on my face, I am stuck crying, again. I did not want to attend the party anymore. My son came into the bedroom and walked over to me. I do not think he noticed any tears, and said excitedly, "Mom please come on, I want to go to mom mom's party, it's getting late!" Literally forcing myself to push past how I feel, I stood up and said, "I have to choose happiness". So, that is exactly what I did and I left for the party with my son.

As I drove in my car to the party, tears still kept flowing from the hurt I felt inside, but I turned the music up loud enough, so that my son would not notice.

While I attended the party, I truly enjoyed myself. I laughed with friends and family. I danced to all the songs that were played. I participated in the family games. It was as if I almost forgot what happened before I arrived. However, I should have known it was only a matter of time before the devil tried to steal my joy again.

From dancing all around my mom's house, I began to sweat. So, I sat down to cool off. When I checked my phone, Gerald had sent text messages to me through an application called Cash App. What person even sends texts' on Cash app?

Apparently, he wanted for me to send him back all the money he had ever given me.

Why can't I just enjoy my day, is what repeatedly went through my mind. Why? At some point, a person can get tired of pushing past their pain.

When Gerlad helped me pay my rent last week, he specified on numerous occasions, you never have to worry about paying me back.

So, I declined his request to receive all his money back, but that did hurt my feelings.

All the years, months, weeks, days, I have had his back. I have never asked him to pay me back anything. How dare he request me to pay him back? How could he be so hurtful? If anything, the way I always provided for him when we lived together, when he faced hardships, he should not be asking for money returned!

All I could do was walk over to the couch my mom happened to be sitting on and sat down next to her. I turned my back from the crowd and began to vent to her before I emotionally broke down. I told my mom the entire situation that occurred before I arrived. She shook her head saying, she was not surprised. However, she believes Gerald's love for me is real, he is just taking the wrong approach to express how he feels. I understood where she was coming from, but I told her I knew when I went back home I would be blue.

As soon as I said that comment, Gerald's younger sister walked over to me and started to vent about her insecurities from her pictures she took recently. Gerald's sister did not know what picture she wanted to post on Instagram. She had not noticed I was crying on the couch with my mom.

The pictures Gerald's sister showed me were gorgeous, but she did not agree.

Gerald's sister and I began laughing at how we are our own biggest critic. The conversation was warm and empowering. We talked and laughed the rest of the evening and I offered to give her a ride home.

While we were riding in the car, she said, "Can I share something personal with you because it seems as if I do not have much to vent to about this situation? If I do not talk to anyone about this I will lose it". So, she opened up about a guy she was dating. I gave her some advice and dropped her off at her home. As soon as she went in the house she called me and said, "Sister, I had to call you back because this conversation was so meaningful." My house is about forty minutes from her house. So while I drove home after dropping her off at her home, Gerald's sister and I stayed on the phone the whole ride. Even when I stepped into my house, we stayed on the phone. When I took the phone off my ear, we had been on the phone for almost two hours.

As I tried to end the conversation, so that I could honestly go into my room and cry my eyes out. Gerald's sister said to me, "Do not give up on Gerald, keep praying for him. You might not see what God is doing for you both, but trust me, God is working on my brother. I know it. All you need is faith."

I knew that God sent her right in the nick of time, because what God intends to work together for my good, the devil wanted me to lose my mind in the process.

Just when the devil thinks he's won by stealing all the joy in my day, God will step in, right on time.

God will send a messenger, which could be a person you'll least expect.

After she spoke those encouraging words to me, I had told her everything that had transpired within the day. She was so shocked. Gerald's sister had no idea that all of this had happened today.

I told her as soon as I told my mother, I'm going to go home and sink in my misery, she walked over to me with a smile. Gerald's sister said, "Wow! God is so amazing because I was all the way across the room and had no idea you were crying. I was honestly looking for someone to vent to about my situation at that moment and said let me walk over to Ebony, she gives great advice."

God truly knows what we need, when we need it.

Instantly when I walked in my home she spoke life right back into me. The peace of God entered my home. I went right to bed with peace and a heart full of joy. The pain I had felt from the entire day went away. I am grateful God used Gerald's sister to help me get through.

Sincerely,
A thankful believer

Chapter 3

PUSHING TO WIN

DAY 3

Dear Diary,   *December 18, 2022*

I had a hard time getting up today. Although I was grateful for Gerald's sister helping me, I still wrestled with my sleep throughout the night. I still longed for a "I love you" text.

The great news is that he did apologize to me this morning. It made me feel better, but I wish I did not have to experience this. Especially when he was just at my house, telling me he wants to be with me. We even managed to try working on our relationship again. Just for our relationship to sink in a hole again.

What really hurts is the games that are played with my heart by Gerald. It's always a repeated cycle of me getting my heart broken while he laughs at the pain.

Nevertheless, I still went into the shower, praised God, and sung out loud the song "We will fight and we will win!" This battle, this war I am in, the devil is defeated and God is exalted. I am a winner! When I stepped out of the shower, I felt renewed. I felt like a conqueror. I am a winner!

I went to church happy, smiling ear to ear. Gerald even texted me while I was in church, "I love you Ebbuwebb". Ebbuwebb is a nickname he gave me. I know, super cute. He actually gave it to me when we first met years ago, when we started off as friends. When he calls me Ebbuwebb, it always lets me know how strong the love remains.

In my mind, I knew things were going to get better from here on out, until he texted saying his Instagram page was hacked. I asked him how? After asking him how, I did not hear from him the rest of the day.

I went to my little cousin's birthday party after church, but did not feel like myself. I honestly knew something was up, but I managed to pray all throughout the day.

When I returned home from the party, God urged me to pray for my father and Gerald's father. Not even realizing both of our fathers have the same first name and both of their last name's start with the letter B. This revealed to me that Gerald and I are connected for a reason.

I interceded for both of our fathers on my knees, the rest of the night. It was through that prayer, I told God I am going to hold on to what he had already promised me.

Sincerely,
Trusting God

Chapter 4

IT'S NOT OVER YET

DAY 4

Dear Diary,   *December 19, 2022*

Today was the absolute worst!

I messed up so horribly.

With Gerald telling me yesterday that someone hacked his page, it had my mind racing. All I continued to think was, did he say this because he's covering something up and changed his password on Instagram?

I paced throughout my apartment, mumbling to myself, "Do not check his Instagram, do not check his Facebook," but eventually I cracked. I logged onto his Instagram account and was curious who he happened to be messaging. I found out that he made several posts, basically letting his followers know he was taken advantage of, in a nutshell. He was also messaging other females and making me overall hurt, once again.

With tears flowing and my body being enraged with anger, I texted him and took my frustrations out on him. My emotions took completely over. The words I used must have been very harsh because this time, he blocked me.

Now initially I just wanted to tell Gerald how I felt in a respectful way. Ultimately, to cut ties with Gerald permanently, but he texted me some screenshots of how much money I owed him, again. Gerald told me he wants me to pay it all back by January 1st. If I did not pay the money back by that date, he needs a new date on when he will receive it. This is over two thousand dollars, that we are referring to.

The tears began to run out my eyes like a running faucet because Gerald knew how expensive my rent was, how I am a single mother, and how I do not ask anyone for help. He offered to help me when he gave me that money for my rent! I never asked him!

I spent my whole entire day miserable.

I called my mom to let her know the situation. She and I began to argue as well. I do not recall why we started to argue, but from my knowledge I knew I was just taking frustrations out on her. My mother did not deserve that.

At this point, I am ready to quit this prayer and fasting journey I am on.

As soon as I told God I quit he sent confirmation that I need to keep holding on. I heard in my spirit, it is not over!

Then I watched a prophetic video that said, "It is not over, until God says, it's over". This woman in the video said, "This battle you are in, God says it's not you. It was never you. It was them. I am working on them. You wanted them to go with you, but I had to take them away from you because I need to work on you and them. Hold on because before you walk into 2023, I am going to bless you publicly. Remember what God told you."

After watching that video, God entered my room, swiftly.

God said, "I told you, in January 2022, that you and Gerald are going to step into a new chapter. I am going to bless you both, more than you can imagine. Gerald is also going to ask you to marry him. The obstacles you both are about to face however, are about to become very challenging. This will be an emotional roller coaster and because of how hard this is going to be, I even understand if you choose to let it all go. If you stay on the ride, I will bless you beyond what you could ever imagine. Your relationship will not just be everything you've always wanted, but it will change the lives of many, through your story."

Now throughout this year of 2022, Gerald has told me a plethora of times that he would like to propose to me. He actually asked me to marry him on my birthday, playfully. Although I knew in his heart he was serious. His family and my family knew the details of the engagement he had planned, but because he lacked the funds, it did not happen.

Hence, in Gerald's phone, he had wedding rings saved in his web browser and pics saved in his photo library. Gerald also took me to the ring store to find out my ring size. Gerald's ring size is eleven and my ring size is nine. Which sounds unbelievable right? Nine eleven, a detrimental day to the world, could likewise mean a detrimental relationship? Right? Wrong. It actually serves a great meaning. I later found out, but that's beside the point.

This year was indeed the most challenging roller coaster I have ever experienced and somewhere, somehow, I lost sight of what God told me.

I kept seeking validation from others when I knew what God told me. Thank God for his messengers who will remind you of what God said.

Not only did that video send confirmation, but so did one of my church members. This church member sent me a video last week. The preacher in the video stated, "Stop talking to people about the situation because they do not know what God told you."

In this season, I feel so alone. Usually I can lean on my mom for guidance and advice, but God told me no! My mom did not see or hear what God told me. In this season, I have to have faith and hope. I have to trust God differently.

God said, "This time, I want you to walk with me on a new path. Trust that I am holding your hand and in December, I am going to bless you with what I promised you back in January. I am not a God that will take you through hard trials, just for you to not receive what I promised you. While you wait on me, I am making and molding you. I am changing you from the inside out. You are almost there. Do not quit! I will always let the enemy think he's doing something, when he's not! I had Gerald and you separate today because the work cannot be done if you communicate with each other at this moment. I did not forget about you Ebony. Hold on. January 1st, Gerald and you are going to walk into your best season ever! You will be walking into your promise!"

Sincerely,
Remembering what he promised me

Chapter 5

GOD'S POWER ACTIVATES
TO BELIEVE

DAY 5

Dear Diary,   *December 20, 2022*

It was a great day!

After I prayed last night, as well as this morning, God spoke to me.

God said, "It is settled, it is finished! Sit back! Pray! Believe! Most importantly, have faith! Wait for it!"

After God spoke, he led me to play the song Never Be Defeated, by Rich Tolbert, Jr., feat. Vincent Bohanan. I began to sing this song out loud. As I sang, I felt victorious. The peace of God that had reigned over me, was now on a higher level.

Since I did not complete my fast correctly, by logging into Gerald's Instagram, I vowed to God. My vow was that I would skip my midnight dinner and not drink anymore ginger ale.

I regained a new level of happiness after committing my vow to God this morning.

I drove my son to school and drove back home.

When I parked my car in front of my home, before I could step out of my vehicle, God told me to play the song, Release Your Power, by James Hall and The Voices of Citadel. As I sat in the car, singing along with the music playing, the song began to resonate in my heart and spirit. Listen, if you are in need of a spiritual healing from God, please play this song. Let it marinate in your mind, body and spirit. I promise, God will enter, wherever you are and give you what you need in the spirit. I truly promise.

After worshiping in my car, I walked into my apartment building still singing the song out loud. It really ministered to me significantly.

When I opened my door to my home, I went to sit at my dining room table.

As I sat at my table, God started speaking once more.

For the past couple of days, my mom has been telling me to watch the movie Polar Express with my son. My mom felt as though the Polar Express movie would get my son and I more engaged in the Christmas spirit.

Now yesterday, I had invited my dad to come over to my home for Christmas Eve. I planned on my dad, my son and I to watch Christmas movies, including Polar Express. However, deep down, I've been so miserable these past couple of weeks. I did not want to watch anything, honestly.

God said to me, "The Polar Express movie's concept is to teach children to believe in the impossible. Christmas is the season to believe. We teach children at an early age to write down what they want for Christmas, to teach them to know what they want and believe their parents, Santa, God, or someone is going to give them the gifts that they have been waiting for. Do you believe Ebony, that I can do what you are asking? Do you believe that I am fixing it? Your problem is, you pray and fear based on how you feel. Based on what you see. Faith is an action word. Faith is believing in what you cannot see. Faith and fear can never coexist. I know based on how your situation looks, what you are asking for seems almost impossible. You cannot believe it because your situation looks different then what I showed you, from when I spoke the promise. I need you to believe that I am going to do what I promised you. Believe it!"

God then instructed me to go in the room and read a book I've been already reading, but stopped a while ago.

Side note, since the beginning of December, God instructed me to read books that are based on controlling your emotions, anger management and prayer guides. I started reading a new book called Master Your Emotions, by Thibaut Meurisse.

As I opened the book and started reading, God said, "I have you reading, taking notes, writing journals, each day because in this season, you are about to help bless, deliver, save, heal and set free others, through your story. Write the book!"

Instantly, with a big smile, I told God yes! God responded, "December 31st, I want you to have an expectation. Have expectations because of your obedience and your faithfulness. Do not doubt and do not expect this to go your way, but expect that I will fulfill my promise to you. I want you to know I am going to blow your mind! Your tears of sorrow will turn into tears of joy! Your praise will be new! Your faith and trust in me will be at a higher level. You are birthing ministry! You are setting yourself up for greatness! 2022 will be your last year crying over Gerald, if you let it. Both Gerald and you are going to embark unto my goodness. Newness is what this season is called for you both!"

After God shared this with me, my heart became filled with gratitude. I cleaned around the house and continued to read my books. Later, I went to pick my son up from school and when I came back home, the gratitude I felt earlier, left. It's unbelievable how God can speak so profoundly and graciously, into us. God will truly empower us. Yet the feelings of doubt come back and take over our bodies.

As I clocked into work on my computer, I told God, "I need you to send confirmation on what I believe I heard you say to me earlier today. Speak to me again oh Lord."

Another side note, God always talks to me in my bathroom for some peculiar reason.

So, I went into my bathroom. Sat on the toilet and waited for God to enter.

I went on YouTube on my phone and a video appeared immediately, titled, it's settled.

The young female in the video said, "God did it. Sit back and wait. God said it's your turn now! Through this year you have pushed past so much pain, heartache, lies, stress and much more. You have given God your all. You fasted and you prayed. You have prayed even when you felt weak, to the point you told God, you could not pray much any longer. God says I remember it all. I watched. I saw your obedience. I saw your faithfulness and because of this, I am going to do it, suddenly. I have you right here, for a reason. It is ok to feel weak, because while you praise me, through your pain, that's when I am going to show right up. I am going to bless you so good, more than you could have ever imagined. Just wait a few more days and see what God is about to do!"

This woman had to be God sent. She was speaking to my entire situation. I literally almost threw my phone across the room, because that word was so prophetic!

As soon as that video was finished, God entered the bathroom and spoke to me.

God said, "Ebony, 2023, will be your last year working for the IRS. It will be your last year working a nine to five job. When you publish this book, I am going to make you into a millionaire."

Listen, God never seizes to amaze me!

I, whole heartedly, love God!

My mother, back on New Year's Day of 2022, prophesied to me. She told me that at her church, out of all the members who were present, I was the millionaire standing in the room. The following Sunday, she made Gerald and I come up to the church altar, for prayer. My pastor went on to say, there was a corporate blessing in the works for us and made us hold hands, while she continued to pray for us.

After that Sunday, God revealed to me that Gerald was going to be my future husband. I just knew 2022 was going to be my best year yet, but it felt like the opposite of what God spoke. In fact, it has been my hardest year yet! From January to September, I carried so much weight. I paid all of my house bills, alone. Jobs continued to not work out for Gerald. The jobs either paid too little or were too far to commute. This caused Gerald and I to argue more and more. Arguments became worse as the months went by. We eventually went to couples counseling. I thought it started to benefit our relationship. Moreover, Gerald and I were baptized together, but every time I thought we were moving forward in the right direction, it felt as if we were moving backwards.

I noticed Gerald changing and not in a beneficial way.

Alcohol started to become an addiction.

Gerald would take his frustrations of how he felt about himself, out on me. Gerald ignored my pain, my tears and my hurt because he felt his pain was louder. I became low inside. I would take Gerald shopping, almost every weekend. I bought Gerald whatever he wanted or needed. I would take him to his favorite restaurants and cover the bills. I would give him my car keys to drive wherever he needed.

It grew to the point, I did not care how much stress was on me. If Gerald was angry with his life, it was my duty to have his back; even when I felt weak. What's sad is, even with this mindset, it still was not enough for Gerald, unfortunately.

Gerald lacked showing me enough appreciation.

2022, I was trying to become the millionaire that God had already destined for me to be. I started a skincare business. I received my LLC and did my due diligence with completing all business documents necessary. I went back to college to receive my degree, but I struggled achieving the A's I wanted; due to focusing on Gerald's wants and needs.

I asked Gerald to try to pick up two jobs to help me out financially and that was a wrestling match. So much tug of war between us both. The level of how much I fasted was insane. I was praying and fasting every other week.

In March of 2022, my pastor insisted I become an intercessor. So, I started taking classes up until graduation in October.

Our class had to read the book Intercessory Prayer by Dutch Sheets, which is a phenomenon. Please go do yourself a favor and read that book. It is life changing! When I read this book, I started to apply what the author, Dutch, teaches, to my life.

Once graduation arrived, for us intercessors at my church, I assumed everything between Gerald and I would be a lot better. It's always wrong to assume.

If anything, it became worse once graduation time came. In fact, we ended our relationship.

The day we ended the relationship, Gerald left our home and the next day I left.

The following day, I blew his phone up with calls and text messages.

I was exhausted from the battle of thinking things would get better when in reality they were not. All Gerald needed to do was stay at a job for a couple of months, but he could not do it. Gerald claims all we have done in our relationship is argue about my money, when in actuality, he is in his pit of misery because of his money, not mine.

After our breakup, I moved back into my mom's house. I was so uncomfortable there! It had nothing to do with me being mistreated. The experience I had was actually the opposite. I had luxury treatment. My mom cooked my son and I dinner each night. My mom would help my son with his homework and look after him if I wanted alone time in my room. She gave me money whenever I asked and so much more. However, I still enjoyed the freedom of having my own and sharing a home with my man.

I went back to Gerald's and my old house almost every night to beg him to fix our relationship. Gerald did not want to fix anything. Gerald began to spread rumors to all of our friends and family that I was the root cause of our breakup and I just accepted it. Internally I had already blamed myself for the suffering in Gerald's and I relationship.

Eventually, after two weeks of living with my mother, God blessed me with a new home in the suburbs. An apartment complex that included a pool, jacuzzi, tennis court, gym, playground and laundry facilities.

It was truly so exciting!

Gerald went with me to my new apartment before I signed all the documents needed to move in. He took a lot of pictures and videos of my place. I believed Gerald was happy for me.

My mom, on the other hand, believed that Gerald captured those pictures and videos of my new home because he could visualize himself living in my apartment with me.

That visual, however, was not Gerald's reality.

Instead, he moved into a tiny room in his sister's basement. This room happened to be his younger brother's room who was only eighteen years old.

Gerald's younger brother had moved out of that room, found a great paying job, found a beautiful new girlfriend, had a precious baby girl with her and moved out.

Gerald's brother even gave his girlfriend a beautiful promise ring.

I could not help to think, how is Gerald's brother only eighteen, doing everything that I begged Gerald to do for years?

As graduation approached for me to become an official intercessor, my pastor and church selected me to be the valedictorian of the class.

I remember saying to myself, "This is something else!" Someone I loved so much, does not love me anymore. Gerald was my best friend for five years before our relationship. Which is why I thought we had the best connection and loved one another so much. What ever happened to what God told me? Hast thou forsaken me?

As these thoughts went into the back of my mind, I could not help but to crack a smile. Then I laughed. In the midst of my storm. Just when I felt as if my life had fallen apart, God would select me to graduate as valedictorian of my intercessory prayer class. God knows how to always remind you of his promise to you!

That same church member, who shared the video with me about remembering what God told me, had told me that Sunday, do not give up on what God told you Ebony.

Ironically, my mom, also referred to as my pastor, has been preaching about the biblical story of Joseph and Joseph's dream. My mom specified in her preaching, how Joseph's dream had not matched his reality.

When God gives you a dream, it's imperative to understand, a storm is about to hit your life. You will not reach your dream, until you get through your storm.

When Gerald and I split, I vented to almost everyone around me, while they continued to confuse me with so many opinions. The confusion only happened because I had to learn to trust God differently. Those around me did not see the version of myself and what God showed me in my dream. The ultimate question God kept asking me was, "Can you get through this trial, only talking to me?"

Later that evening, God told me "You have now passed your training! From the beginning of January until the end of September, I birthed out of you, what I showed you in your dream. You had thought I ordained you to become an intercessor for the glitz and glam, or because it sounds cool? No! I am going to allow you to walk into your divine calling with a purpose! You are going to be able to help others that are amongst you, birth what they need from me, out of prayer! I had you become valedictorian because now, you are ready! You did not quit, no matter how many stones were thrown at you. You may have grown to become tired, weary, and even frustrated at me, but you trusted me past these feelings. I have seen all the tithes and the offerings you have sown into the kingdom. You have never missed a Sunday! I have heard every prayer! I saw your continuous effort to fast when times grew hard. I adored your worship, your praise, and how you served me with gladness! It is a joy to witness all the individuals you have helped give their life to me! Which is why in this next coming year, this is going to be the best year you have ever experienced in your life! My only question to you now is, where is your faith? The storm is almost over and you are almost at the finish line! Keep your faith uplifted! Watch how the blessings are about to fall! On December 31ˢᵗ, I promise you, you will be amazed at what I am going to do for you! Just watch! Now write the book. Follow every assignment I will give to you and watch me work!"

Sincerely,
Holding On To His Promise

Chapter 6

DREAMS TO FOLLOW GOD'S WILL

DAY 6

Dear Diary,   *December 22, 2022*

Today was simply amazing! I've been staying in God's presence! This relationship, God and I have been developing, has been tremendously wonderful.

While I drove back home this morning, from dropping my son off to school, I began thinking about a dream God gave me last night. Let me tell you all the backdrop to why God gave me this dream.

Last week, Gerald and I were able to get into a great place again in our relationship. We were able to mend a lot of our differences. Gerald had paid my rent. He also took me on a few romantic dates, and scheduled an appointment to get my hair done. Gerald was truly going the distance and putting me on cloud nine. As elated as I was, I was still upset with myself.

About two weeks before Gerald and I rekindled what we once had, I vowed to myself that I would complete a ninety-day self-love fast. The goal of this fast was to heal myself. I needed a spiritual cleansing. A part of my self-love fast, was not to communicate with Gerald, within this ninety-day window. God had confirmed to me, this self-love fast, was indeed, necessary.

So, the night before the start date of my self-love fast, I called Gerald. I called him just to say farewell. I told Gerald about the fast and his reaction was quite devastating. I felt horrible from how he expressed how miserable he would be without speaking to me for so long. By the end of that night, we had stayed on our phone call the entire day and he arrived at my house later that night. He spent the night and never left.

The nice gestures Gerald was doing for me were splendid, however I knew I was not being obedient to God's will.

Immediately when reality hit that I needed to be obedient to God, God said to me, "Ebony, if you do this your way, you will be temporarily happy now, but ultimately you are going to only hurt yourself. A greater level of sadness will come, if you continue following this through, your way."

It was frustrating that God said this because Gerald had specified that he wanted us to be together again. Hence, the fact that I could see a huge change in him. God said to me, "I know how you are feeling, because he is almost ready to become the man you want him to be. However, you must do this my way! If you are obedient, you may feel temporarily hurt now, but you will enter a season full of happiness, wealth and joy, that you have not experienced before." I told God, with an attitude, "Fine! Your way it is!" I left it at that. The reality is, this is about to be a hard decision. One important fact that we should know is that God loves when we make challenging decisions! Hard decisions are the biggest test of our faith in God.

I felt like I cannot just tell Gerald to leave, when he's doing everything to keep me afloat and happy. How dare I just say, I cannot talk to you because I am doing a fast for God and myself? Gerald would feel like this is why we ended the relationship; all because of Ebony. So, in the end, I still chose my way.

Literally the next day, after having that conversation with God, Gerald switched up, quicker than a light switch being flicked on. Gerald asked me the next morning, when can you take me back home with a frustrated tone. I was confused. Gerald had set out plans for us to have date nights for the rest of the week. Why cancel our plans so soon? That is all I kept asking myself. I told Gerald, with a soft tone, "I am not sure".

Gerald grew distant from me. He did not even look in my direction when we were in the same room. He always insisted on sleeping on the couch. That weekend, I left my apartment to take my son to get his haircut. While I waited for the barber to finish cutting my son's hair, I called Gerald. When Gerald answered I asked him, "Once I drop you off today, when will you be coming back over?" Gerald's response was "I do not know, maybe in a few weeks." Instantly my emotions overwhelmed me. We had already made a pact to visit one another every weekend, while still periodically visiting one another throughout the week. For Gerald to switch up so quickly, I knew something secretive was up.

As soon as I came back home from taking my son to the barber, Gerald had all his bags packed and ready to go home, at the door. I stormed into my bathroom, slammed the bathroom door and burst out into tears. Gerald had just told me everything was going to be better. Our relationship would be different. Gerald kneeled on his knees to me, grabbed my hand and said, "I'm aiming to become a better man for you, for us!" How can someone make all these efforts to attempt to fix what was broken, just to shatter it more?

Due to me teleworking and working the night shift, I told him I could not take him home until midnight. Hours went by. I managed to gather my thoughts. I stepped away from my workstation and sat next to Gerald on my couch. I told Gerald, "You know, you do not have to force yourself to be with me, if you are not ready. I could feel the vibes changing. Immediately he responded, stating "Ebony, I want to be single. I enjoy not having to answer to anyone and having my freedom."

Hearing Gerald's response had hurt my heart deep, but I held back my tears. More than anything, I was quite baffled. A man does not come back into a relationship, just to turn back around and leave again. Maybe men do. I am not sure. I just know that something is definitely off. I could sense it because Gerald just filled my refrigerator with groceries yesterday morning. It's simply not adding up.

I had to tell Gerald he was being misleading.

Of course, Gerald gave the typical immature response, replying, "I never intended on being back together right now. I did not ask to come over. I never forced you into anything." It's sadly, the average, immature, male response.

I grabbed my phone and showed him the beautiful, happy pictures we have taken this week. I said, "If that is the case Gerald, explain your happiness in these pictures!"

Gerald turned his head at me, looked me directly in my eyes and said,

"Ok Eb, I will be honest with you. You are most certainly the woman I want to be married to. I want you to have my children. I want to travel the world with you. It's just that, I am not in the right position to provide for you, the way I would like to. No woman should be accepting a man with no car, while she has a car. She also has an apartment, two government jobs, in college full time and overall, has a lot going for herself. Meanwhile, her man lives in his sister's basement. In a tiny room without windows, with no job. To top it all, I am unhappy with the weight that I have been gaining. I cannot even afford a haircut most of the time. When I leave here, I plan to grind harder with my life. I need to fix my situation, so I can take care of my stepson and you. If you want to date new men, as much as I would not want them to even look your way, I want you to be happy. I truly love you Ebony, beyond what you think. I know you have seen females and disturbing things in my phone, but I promise, you are the only person on my mind every second of the day. I only want you. When I return home today, my social media might have you fooled, but I promise, I am fixing myself for you. No female, no person on earth, has my heart, the way you do. Let me become the new Gerald for you. Let me become the new Gerald for us!"

Side note, my pastor prophesied to Gerald last Sunday and told him he's closer to becoming the new Gerald that he wants to be. So, I believe he is making great attempts to become a new version of himself.

Listening to Gerald pour out his heart felt so refreshing. I've always known that Gerald's love for me was real. Honestly, it's why I still have hope.

After that conversation the energy in the room was more peaceful. Gerald and I laughed, chatted, watched movies, cuddled and were intimate. Gerald did not go home. While we were asleep in bed that night, God gave me a dream. This is the dream that I was referring to in the beginning of this chapter.

The dream started with me being on a private island vacation.

Well, actually, Gerald, my best friend and my best friend's ex-boyfriend. My best friend and her boyfriend were sitting next to Gerald and I in the beach chairs. My best friend and her ex-boyfriend were still not together in my dream.

So, while Gerald and I were cuddled up being romantic, they were not.

Suddenly my best friend was upset with her ex-boyfriend because he was not paying her any attention. Instead of showing my best friend attention, he ex-boyfriend called another female on FaceTime in front of us all. Gerald and I were confused. I personally felt bad. I could tell Gerald did too. Surprisingly, my best friend was nonchalant about it. It was obvious that she was used to her ex-boyfriend dealing with other women. I am not sure if my best friend being unbothered attracted her ex-boyfriend because shockingly, he picked her up in his arms and carried her into a private room. He had caressed her body, kissing and mumbling sweet things in her ear. While my best friend enjoyed every minute of it. I shook my head in disbelief. I just knew that what they were doing was wrong and I did not want her hurting her own heart in the end.

After my best friend and her boyfriend took off, I could not find Gerald. I only remembered Gerald telling me he would come right back, but somehow, he did not. So, as we returned home, I put out a search warrant for Gerald to all of my friends. My best friend, who was in charge of this warrant, promised that Gerald would be found.

My anxiety was at an all-time high because Gerald was supposed to pick my son up from school when we arrived back from the vacation.

The odd part about this dream was that my mom called me stating that my son was fine with her. However, I received multiple calls from my son's school saying he was still there and needed to be picked up. I even remembered in this dream, I picked my son up from school, but I couldn't remember if he was still with his teacher in class. This caused me to panic.

I called my best friend and she said everyone is looking for Gerald. She insisted that I should only focus on myself and my son. Gerald would be found. I ignored her, since I still did not receive any updates.

While I went on a rampage search to find Gerald, my head was spinning.

Eventually my best friend and my other friends met up with me at a playground. I told my friends that I was becoming light headed, running all around town, to find my boyfriend.

My friends wiped off the sweat on my head with a tissue, handed me a cold bottle of water, and said, "Relax Eb".

While I sat down, hoping to get my body at ease, my best friend walked over to a bush and screamed, "I found him!" My eyes became so wide, they almost popped out of my face.

I looked over and there Gerald was. He was in the bushes, doing inappropriate things with some woman.

Can you imagine how humiliated I was? To think I would run miles all around town, while he calls himself hiding, but in reality, publicly embarrassing me! I had no words to say.

I left immediately.

When I left the island to look for Gerald, I left my phone on the beach chair.

While I walked away feeling pitiful, my best friend yelled, "Ebony we can go back with you to the island, to get your phone, so you can pick up your son!" I responded, "Nope, it's fine!", with my head hanging down, still walking away. Gerald yelled out to me, "I thought you already knew where I was based off my Instagram page? I still did not look back.

I continued walking.

As the tears rolled down my face, I just kept walking. I walked for hours. I walked for days. The days kept changing and I still kept walking.

I remember asking strangers if I could use their phones for directions to where I was heading. I was explaining to them that I needed to find my son. Everyone I asked told me no.

As I continued walking, I asked a lady if I could give her money. I asked in hopes that she would get me an Uber to my destination because my feet were hurting. She also said no.

I still kept walking.

I stopped again to ask another woman if I could use her phone to check my social media pages. This woman, again, told me no.

So, I continued walking once more. The more I walked, the tears faded away. All the no's I was receiving, made me determined to find my own way, alone. I did not need a phone, a bicycle, a car, or a bus. It was no longer about getting to my destination quickly. Although I knew I was closer to wherever it was that I needed to be.

The more I encouraged myself, as I walked, my frown turned into a smile. My worrying turned into joy. I started laughing at my own jokes I would tell myself as I walked. This joy made me lift my head up and look more clearly for where I was going.

As I looked up, I found an area where the taxis were to arrive. In the area, there was only one more taxi left. I ran to the area, as fast as I could. I waved my hand to get the taxi driver's attention. I yelled, "Please wait!" He smiled at me and opened the car door for me.

When I sat down in the taxi and the driver took off, we both smiled at one another through the rear-view mirror. My smile was because I was relieved I no longer had to walk. I was not sure where his smile derived from. I told him the address I was going to and asked him if he knew where this was. The taxi driver responded, "Nope, but you can show me if you'd like." I looked at the driver with a small grin and said, "Well, that is fine with me." Suddenly I woke up from the dream.

When I woke up from the dream, I sat up on my bed and I held my heart tight. The dream ended well, I guess, but it felt so real; too real.

The pain I felt in the dream when I saw Gerald in the bushes, was still in my heart once I woke up. I felt those tears that I cried. That feeling of being alone was in my dream, entering my room. As I tried to grasp all of the emotions I felt from my dream, I realized I had no one to call on, but God.

Have you ever been in a situation that had you so hurt and God made sure of it, that you would walk through it alone? Well, not necessarily alone, but just you and God.

After my emotions had calmed down, I went into my living room and kneeled on my knees, before the Lord. I asked God to please not allow that dream to happen, not knowing the dream would eventually come true.

So, as I am driving home, from picking my son up from school, back to the beginning of this chapter, I thought about this dream. This dream was so meaningful to my current situation. Although, I still do not fully understand the role Gerald played in this dream. I guess, the ultimate question is, should I still hold on? What if the man driving the taxi, in my dream, was the man that was meant for me? What if the man in the taxi was the new Gerald? What if the man driving the taxi was God? My mind continued wondering, who was this man? Who was the taxi driver in my dream? At least, the great part about my dream is, I understood most of it.

My perspective of my dream was, God wanted me not to worry about my son. God wanted to give me reassurance that son is well cared for. God wants me to pray for my best friend's situation.

By the way, my best friend was in fact in a similar situation in real life. God told me to not judge her, but to keep her close to me because she would help me get through my situation; which in fact, she did.

God wanted me to know, Gerald may think he is hiding, but he's only fooling himself. Whatever Gerald is hiding will be on public display.

God wants me to stop seeking others for answers, like I did in my dream.

God wants me to eliminate my phone, silencing social media and my friends.

What I asked myself after evaluating this is, "How is this going to demonstrate if this is in God's will for Gerald and I to be together?" I know God told me so much about Gerald and I being back together again, but my dream showed the opposite. Now I am confused.

Then God uttered to me, "Why? When you woke up, you were never able to see where the taxi took you. You allowed your emotions to take over and lose sight. Which should remind you of the book I have you reading about, Controlling Your Emotions. If you do not learn to control your emotions, you will lose a lot of blessings that I have in store for you. When you entered the taxi, you told the driver your destination. Which is why I told you, "Nope, I do not know where that is at, but you can show me". I told you no, because you are not going where you want to go when you come with me. You will go where I want you to go. I stated, "You can show me", because the reality is, I'll always let you think that you know where it is that you are going to, but my will, will always be done! On earth, as it is in heaven! I am letting you know I will always take you where you need to go. There is a difference between an Uber and a taxi. An Uber shows you a route on your phone and a taxi goes the route he knows best, without using navigation devices. When you ride in a taxi, you have to just trust the taxi knows where he is going, once you give him the address."

Not only did God reveal all these things to me, but he always showed me how I was walking into the promise land. The moment I found the taxi and the moment the taxi driver opened the car door for me, was the moment God opened the door to my promise. God sent confirmation that I was entering into my new beginning!

Before God spoke these words to me, I battled with taking Gerald home, but after I received this prosperous word, I took Gerald home immediately.

God will always give us a choice. In this decision process, I chose victory! Not my way anymore and no more delays to what God promised me! I have to let God do his work and walk with him.

The next day, as I sat in my car, I said, "God I need to pray for Gerald on a deeper level now. I will choose to get closer to this promise." God said, "Ok, then go watch his YouTube channel and all of his videos he has uploaded on his social media." So, I did just that. I went home, walked into my bedroom and sat on my bed, watching his videos. I grabbed a notebook and pen to take notes of what I saw. While I watched Gerald's videos of himself, I noticed so much that I had not noticed before. I wrote everything I evaluated down and fell asleep in my notebook.

Once I fell asleep, I fell into a powerful dream from God. In my dream, I was swimming in the ocean, not too far from shore. I enjoyed swimming so much that I suddenly became an expert. I fell in love with swimming in the ocean. My passion for swimming in the ocean grew to me swimming under the sea. It was almost as if I had become a mermaid or Aqua-man, preferably, Aqua-woman.

As I swam under sea, I started to look for friends, since I had seemed to be the only human under sea. While I looked and looked, another human came up to me from behind, tapped my shoulder, and asked to be friends. With a burst of excitement, I said, "Yes! Absolutely!"

I should have been more attentive when choosing this man to be my friend because I had no idea of what his appearance was. I just knew I needed a friend. This friend told me his name was Bruce.

Bruce and I would swim with each other every day under the sea, all throughout the ocean. We always had an amazing time. Bruce showed me so much, throughout the sea. I was safe with him. Bruce and I had become best friends. Until one day, trouble hit the waters.

A shark came and began attacking everyone in the water. All the creatures under the sea vanished. I could not find Bruce anywhere! I feared he may have been eaten by the shark! People in the water and at the beach shore were screaming. Everyone was swimming as fast as they could, to return to the beach shore. Although I was terrified, I had to find Bruce. My friends that came to the beach with me, were on the beach shore, screaming, "Ebony get out of that water!" While I swam like a cheetah running in the jungle, my friends screamed even louder. They said, "Ebony! The Shark is right behind you!" Now, I am swimming even faster and the shark was so close to me, that it bit my foot! Everyone on shore and my friends are going bananas, screaming louder than a fire truck siren! I turned my head back, looking at the shark in its eyes and screamed to the top of my lungs, "Get off my foot!" Surprisingly, the shark let my foot go, but it still followed, even when I made it to the beach shore. With the shark now being out of the water, the beach had turned into a madhouse! Everyone was in a panic, including me! What made my blood boil, higher, was that even though the shark let my foot go, the shark only seemed to chase me on the beach shore. The shark was not chasing anyone else, although everyone was still in fear. The shark only chased me! When I looked at my foot however, there was no scar and no blood. I do not think my friends noticed when the shark had bit me because no one asked if my foot was hurt.

My friends and I had found a safe place to huddled up at.

One of my friends had mentioned, "This is all confusing." I said, "What is confusing?"

Another friend answered and said, "Why is the shark only chasing you? We're running for no reason!" My response was "We're running because this is terrifying! Did you all see this shark bite my foot?" Everyone mumbled, No, I did not see that happen. I do not recall."

One of my other friends said, "Why would the shark bite you if you were not in the ocean."

I'm assuming that my friends did not remember me swimming in the ocean, at all! So, because of their confusion, I was now confused.

I felt completely lost.

How could my friends forget what I just endured? How is it that they can only identify that the shark only wants me? Are my friends trying to sacrifice me? I know they are uncomfortable and afraid, but I am their friend for goodness sake or maybe I'm not! Fear can change people.

So, I left my friends and ran off.

If my friends do not want to come together to make an executive decision on how we are going to eliminate this shark, then I will move accordingly on my own!

As soon as I left the safe place, the shark came following me! I ran as far as I could.

While I ran, I approached a parking lot. In the lot, I saw some teenagers that were chilling in a yellow jeep.

In the driver's seat was a young man and in the passenger seat was his girlfriend. The girlfriend had her passenger door left open. Their friends were standing outside of the jeep.

When I saw the shark was not too far behind me, I pulled the girlfriend out of the jeep, pushed her, slammed the car door and locked the doors. I screamed to the young man in the driver's seat, "Drive off now!"

The girlfriend of this young man and his friends were yelling, "Hey, who are you? What are you doing? What in the world is wrong with you?"

Then immediately they turned their heads around and saw the shark coming. They all started panicking and took off running.

The young man in the driver's seat sped the car off.

I could tell the shark grew angrier when it saw I was in a car with this young man.

The shark started damaging all the cars in the parking lot.

I did not care, I was elated, I was able to find a way of escape!

The young man did not drive too far, since he worried about his girlfriend and his friends.

The young man drove up to a mountain cliff and we found a cave to camp in, about two miles from the beach.

Due to the mountain cliff being so high, I could still see the shark searching around on the beach. Everyone on the beach changed. No one seemed frightened by the shark anymore. As the sun went down, the beach was peaceful. I saw the girlfriend of the young man who drove me in his jeep, saying, "How could she just throw me out of my boyfriend's car? How did I let her do it? They're probably cuddling right now!" I never did anything inappropriate with the young man in the jeep. In fact, we barely talked. He was definitely a cool dude, but we did not like one another in that magnitude. The young man told me how much he had loved his girlfriend.

After a while, I laid down in the cave to take a nap. I woke up around one o' clock in the morning and sat on the cliff. As I sat on the cliff, I still found this day to be so strange. How is it that now, it's past midnight, a shark is on the beach and everyone is so calm? Everyone on the beach could see the shark, but because the shark was not attacking anyone, they could go on about their day. As I stared into deep thought, the shark approached me. I ran into the cave I was camping in. The young man who drove me up this hill, in his jeep, was nowhere to be found. When I entered the cave, I became a tiny clown fish. The shark came to the cave and said to me, "I am sorry for attacking you. I am sorry for causing so much trouble. The truth is, I have loved you since I first saw you in the ocean, swimming alone. I have watched you closely, every day, since you came into the ocean. I loved everything about you and I was afraid that you would reject me. So, I swam with you as a human so that you could notice me, but once you grew close to me, I could not hide for much longer. I never meant to bite your foot. I just did not want you to leave once you saw the real me. I am still very much in love with you. I did not eat you or those people on the beach because I still have a good heart. I just can not control that being a shark is in my nature." Then the shark swam away.

I know in my heart that the shark did not leave me. I yelled out "Bruce, wait, I love you also!" The shark did not return. Tears filled my eyes. I went back into the cave and cried my eyes to sleep. While I was talking to the shark, I remember everyone on the beach, looking up at us. They were murmuring, "How in the world could she be communicating with a shark? Is she not afraid?" I knew who Bruce was. He appears as a shark, but he's not harmful.

I had hope that Bruce would return. My heart told me that he would. Around six o' clock am, Bruce had returned. Bruce said to me, "I love you, let's go back and swim." We left. As Bruce was still a shark and I was still a clown fish; we swam back into the ocean. Then I woke up.

Immediately after I woke up from this dream, I googled shark characteristics. A few characteristics were:

- *sharks have great tunnel vision,*
- *Sharks rarely attack humans,*
- *sharks eat primarily fish,*
- *sharks have been in the ocean for generations,*
- *Sharks have the same feelings and emotions as humans*
- *Sharks are silent hunters*

- *Sharks have skin like sandpaper*
- *Sharks do not have bones*
- *Sharks weakest sense is taste*
- *Sharks become depressed due to poor feeding*
- *Sharks cannot cry*
- *Sharks are afraid of bright colors, they prefer dark colors*
- *Sharks are afraid of whales*

Whales are the most dominant creatures of the sea. Wow! Listen, this amazed me deeply. Gerald matched all the characteristics of a shark. I could explain every detail of how Gerald embezzles himself as a shark, but I am not. The revelation I received from this dream was that Gerald hid who he was from me because he truly believed I would not accept him. The truth is you can run, but you cannot hide.

My mom has been on a teaching series at church about speaking to the nature of a person. When you know a person's nature you do not speak at it, you speak to it.

After hearing many sermons on this topic, I asked God to reveal to me Gerald's true nature and how to speak to it. However, overtime when Gerald and I would argue, I always found myself speaking at him and not to him.

So, after having this dream and grasping the message God sent, I thanked God for being faithful. I still asked God, "Why a shark?" God said, "Where you are headed, you are about to swim with many sharks. You are not going to know how to deal with them, if you have never experienced dealing with a shark."

Then instantly I remembered, earlier this year, my mom kept telling Gary and I to watch the Shark Tank television show. My mom wanted Gerald and I to learn how to profit from businesses.

Every time Gerald and I would visit my mom, she always had on *Shark Tank* television show. My mom even prophesied to me at church one Sunday and said, "Ebony, God said, "You think you are only going to have one business, when you are going to have multiple business. God showed me you sitting with sharks, investing in other businesses. I even saw you becoming a shark having multiple businesses."

So, I told God, now this all makes perfect sense. God will always prepare you for the table you were always meant to sit at, even if it is with predators.

Gerald is going to protect me from the sharks that will try to bite me. God said, "Ebony I made you a fish for a reason. In the movie Finding Nemo, the main character, the clown fish, had to encounter sharks, whales, jellyfish, even birds to find his missing son. The clown fish was never eaten by any of those creatures. He may have been attacked, but he had power that he did not know existed, until he had to go on a journey to find his son. That clown fish, is you. Where I am taking you, the sharks will want what is yours, but they cannot have it. Your power will come, when you learn to speak to its nature!" I told God, "Where in my life, am I at, like in this dream? God said, "You are close to the end."

After this conversation with God, I left to go pick up my son from school. As I am driving in my car, singing gospel music, Gerald texts me. As soon as I arrived home, Gerald called me, twice. I did not respond to his text or his calls. A part of me really wanted to respond, but another part of me wanted to be prideful.

So, I prayed.

God had already revealed to me that Gerald would return back, but I did not know it would be this quickly. I texted him after I prayed and said, "Hey." I received no response. Hours went on, still no response.

Since Gerald was not responding, I walked into my bathroom, looked at myself in the mirror, and began to cry.

After a few tears were shed, God spoke to me swiftly, allowing me to barely cry the way I intended to.

God said, "Ebony, why are you crying? You are at the finish line with this battle. For all the months you have carried this relationship, I was birthing something great out of you! In January, of 2022, I gave you the promise and sent reminders throughout each month leading up till now. You were pregnant with your promise. I had to make you walk, like the doctors make pregnant women do before labor, so that they can start dilating. I had needed you to dilate, so that you could push out your promise!"

In my intercessory class, back in May, of 2022, we had an assignment called, praying until you push. I thought the assignment was creative, but I did not realize it was preparation for me to push out what I've been pregnant with. God said to me, "What I have for you is here, but just like when a new mommy has to readjust her life with a newborn, you have to readjust right now and keep going. In the dream you recently had, you were at the end of the battle you've faced for months. You were waiting for Bruce to return. While you wait for Gerald to return, go get ready because he is coming. Clean your house. Fix up your hair. Put on a beautiful outfit. Gerald will be here soon."

It is now twelve o' clock in the morning. A new day, but no response still. A little voice told me to play a popular church chant from Bethel Temple. A part of the lyrics to this chant says, "I've seen him do it and I know he is working it out for me. It's getting ready to happen." These words gave me hope! These words gave me joy! I know God's going to do it!

I woke up again at three o' clock in the morning. I still received no response. So, I blocked Gerald and I cried. I told God, "I do not get it. In my dream, Gerald came before the sun came up, why is he still not responding? Why tell me to go get ready?" Then, I went back to sleep.

It is now five o' clock in the morning. I told God, "It is almost dawn. The sun will come up at seven o' clock." I know this because I wake up everyday around 5 o' clock in the morning to pray and at 6 o'clock, I'm usually getting dressed so that I can take my son to school.

After I finished praying at six o' clock am, I went back into my bedroom to check my phone. Gerald had texted me from a text free phone number, sending me about eight long messages. I smiled with joyful tears rolling down my face. God is always true to his word! Hours later, Gerald showed up to my house.

If God said it will happen, it will happen. I have seen him do it and I know that he is working it out for you! Just wait on it because it's getting ready to happen!

Sincerely,
Always Trusting God

Chapter 7

THE WRONG PATH

DAY 7

Dear Diary,   *December 23, 2022*

I cannot believe Gerald is here.

Literally, as soon as Gerald arrived, we were loving all over one another. We had missed each other so much.

Seeing Gerald, felt magical.

Gerald had told me that he had not slept in days.

In the back of mind, all I could think was, God had me praying and fasting for Gerald with a purpose. Every time I prayed for Gerald, the Lord showed me Gerald being on a surgery table. God was the doctor and I was the nurse. God said, "Through your prayers for Gerald, I am performing surgery on him. When I finish the surgery, he will return. Gerald's recovery process, after surgery, will not be easy. Stick to your fast to have a great outcome. You are in charge of how Gerald heals."

So, when Gerald told me that he had not slept in days, I hugged him tightly, while smiling. I told him to go lay down in my bed. We both laid down, cuddled, and went to sleep.

I wanted to stay committed to my fast, but the temptation of wanting to snoop on Gerald's phone was haunting me. I could not resist. I took Gerald's phone while he was sleeping and identified that Gerald had changed his password. I had the old password memorized. Now I am really forced to search on his phone.

Nothing I tried worked. I woke Gerald up, to call my phone, pretending I had lost my phone. I tried asking him if I could use his phone, but he kept asking why, so that did not work either. I attempted to take his phone while he was sleeping and tried to figure out his passcode. Eventually I was locked out of his phone for one hour. So, I had quit trying to find out what was in his phone.

I went to cook us both a lovely dinner. I cleaned around my house and then I climbed back into my bed, holding Gerald tightly. I laid with him daydreaming about our beautiful future together. Then Gerald woke up. I stood up and walked towards the bedroom door, so that I could go back into the kitchen to check on the food I was cooking.

Gerald woke up smiling from ear to ear. He told me that he had not slept this good in days. I could also see the excitement in his face, knowing I was cooking dinner for us both. He looked at me and said "You're cooking?" I said, "Yes, I can tell you needed a great meal." This made Gerald smile even harder. Gerald said, "I am so excited."

By the way, Gerald thinks I should be a world-renowned chef. He loves when I cook dinner.

After Gerald told me how excited he was to eat dinner, he looked at me deep into my eyes, almost piercing my soul. Gerald still had a smile on his face, but the stare was awkward. He said "Come here baby." So, I came and sat on my bed next to him. Gerald said, "Did you try hacking into my phone again?" I responded, "No, I do not know what you are talking about." Gerald said, "Are you sure?" I gave up telling lies and said, "Ok, fine, yes I tried hacking your phone and I am sorry!" Gerald laughed and said, "Why would you want to do that? I am not hiding anything from you."

I felt ashamed that Gerald caught me. So, I changed the topic of the conversation and said, "Let's go watch tv, dinner is almost ready." While Gerald and I were picking out a show to watch, I asked Gerald if we were going to spend Christmas with one another, as well as New Year's Eve. Gerald told me due to us already being at odds, he had already made plans to spend the holidays with his cousin. I heard God telling me to not get upset, do not make this into my way or I will mess up what I worked for and prayed for, with Gerald.

I tried to listen. I tried to the best of my ability, but eventually we started arguing over why he should be spending the holidays with me and we were at odds, again. I could not express my feelings to Gerald, without him seeming upset, so I stormed out of the room, slamming the door.

While I tried to cool off in my living room, Gerald started blasting Christmas songs from my bedroom television. Gerald yelled from the bedroom, "Eb come dance with me." I had too much pride. I ignored him and walked into my bathroom to pray. Gerald followed me, so I locked the bathroom door. Gerald yelled, "Why are you locking the door?" Then he walked back into the bedroom and sang along to the Christmas carols that were playing still on my television.

As I sat in the bathroom, I said, "God, I want to be obedient, but it is hard. Why would Gerald not want to spend the holidays with me?" I kept praying. I wanted answers from God. God was not speaking, but I told God, "Your will be done!"

I prayed for about fifteen more minutes and went back into the bedroom with Gerald. I apologized to Gerald, sincerely. He grabbed my hand and said "Eb, I love you. Stop picking the wrong times to have certain conversations. I understand that you have feelings, but we were having a great time. We could have came back to that conversation at a different time, if we disagreed." This was in fact true, but I still wanted my way. I also felt like he was trying to pin the argument on me, so I told him he was wrong. This made Gerald get frustrated and go outside on my patio to get some air.

Since he walked outside, I texted him and told him, "I can just take you back home now." He came back into my apartment and said, "Ok I can go home whenever you are ready." In the blink of an eye, it was now two o' clock in the morning and we were in a screaming match. We were not even listening to one another, just screaming. I started crying and Gerald walked over to me and wiped my tears away. He hugged me and said, "Stop crying Ebbuwebb."

It's Christmas Eve and we are not getting along. It is the greatest time of the year and yet it does not feel like Christmas at all. How can God want me to believe this Christmas when I feel defeated.

Gerald grabbed my hand and I followed him back into my bedroom.

Gerald said to me, "Let's stop this madness and go back to spending quality time with each other." I responded, "Ok."

I forced a smile, but in reality, I was still upset. I was mad at myself more than anything. I was mad at myself for not being obedient. God not only told me to stop trying to do things my way, but he also told me to control my emotions. I did not do either. God told me at that moment, "You have to finish your book you're reading about controlling your emotions, or else, you are going to block your own blessings."

Here I am, once again. I am forced to try to move past yet another argument. All because I could not control my emotions.

Sincerely,
A disobedient believer

Chapter 8

THE PAST AFFECTS THE PRESENT

DAY 8

Dear Diary,   *December 24, 2022*

Did I mention my mom's dream to you all?

My mom called me yesterday, while I was in the car with Gerald. She told me she had a dream about me. In the dream, my mom stated, I gave her a large sum of money and asked her if she could hold it for me. I happened to be going on a business trip.

Before I left for this business trip, Gerald came in a nice car, begging for me to get in. I ignored him at first, but eventually ended up getting in the car and leaving with Gerald.

My mom mentioned how in the dream Gerald mentioned how he was such a better person, but I kept looking out the window.

This morning when I woke up all I could think about was my mom's dream. I was not sure why this was on my mind though.

I left out early this morning to get Christmas gifts for everyone. Gerald stayed back at my apartment to get ready to go to his cousin's house.

While I was shopping at the mall, I could not help to hear how everyone around me was talking about how they could not wait to spend the holidays with their loved ones. I kept thinking about how this would be my first Christmas, in a while, that I would not be spending with Gerald, but I did my best to push past how I felt.

When I arrived back home, I could tell something was bothering Gerald, but I did not ask.

While we were riding in the car, he was extremely quiet. This is not like Gerald. Usually in our car rides, Gerald is asking "What would you prefer, this or that?", or he's asking an unbelievable and hypothetical question that would probably make you cringe internally. He's known for starting conversations that turn into debates. However, Gerald remained quiet.

I did not like the quietness, so I turned on a Christmas playlist on my phone, in hopes it would help us to feel holly jolly. Gerald lightened up a little, but his energy was still off.

Once I had dropped Gerald off to his destination and left to continue Christmas shopping, I waited for Gerald to send his usual, "Get there safely sweetheart" text messages. I did not receive one. Two hours, three hours passed, and still no text.

As my Christmas shopping was close to an end, I called to see if he wanted me to buy him anything from the mall. I called three times. No one answered. Gerald called me back thirty minutes after I called three times. When I answered, my feelings of sadness took over my body.

While Gerald and I were chatting, I tried to not mention how I felt.

I told Gerald that I wanted to buy him something from the mall. He gave a dry response saying, "I do not need anything". Then there was a long awkward silence on the call. I told him how excited I was to see everyone's reaction to what I bought them. Gerald, still being dry, responded, "Ok" and that was it. I asked him if there was something wrong. He told me nothing was wrong. That was the last straw for me. I blacked out. I told him, "It feels as though you are unsure if you're ready to be in a relationship again. It's almost as if you want to be single, but you are still attached to me. You do not want me to move forward with my life, but you also do not want to be forced into a relationship. It is so selfish! You know a woman loves you and you take advantage of the love I have for you."

I began to cry. I did not like the fact that I had to experience these emotions on Christmas Eve.

Christmas Eve may feel like a regular day to some, but Christmas season is my absolute favorite time of the year.

You know what Gerald's response was, after I had cried my eyeballs out?

Gerald said, "You're right. I do not know what it is that I want. I do know I enjoy being single. I enjoy having my freedom. Not having to check in consistently with you is a great feeling. However, I love you beyond words could describe. I still see you as my future wife, having all my children. I just do not know when I will be ready to be the man you want me to be and I do not want you waiting around for me for that simple fact. I need to work on myself and so do you. There's no telling how long that will take, but I will like to remain friends. I will still come over after the holidays to spend time with you."

Can you all believe this? This man begged me to love him again. He literally poured his heart out to me, on a text free app because I had him blocked. He called me numerous times, asking if he could see me. He expressed to me how he wanted the relationship back. Gerald promised me that we were building and working on us.

Once Gerald expressed that he had wanted to be single, I immediately blacked out. Enraged with anger, I started yelling and screaming. The feelings of being used, manipulated and betrayed, all consumed me.

I was hurt.

Gerald's response to my anger was, "I do not know why you are feeling this way. I never told you that we were back into a relationship again. I only expressed what I wanted for our future."

Is this not manipulation at its finest?

Gerald and I argued for three hours straight. Gerald was yelling and so was I. For three complete hours. It's strange right?

In the fourth hour however, the argument drifted.

Gerald started confessing where he falls short as a man. He spoke about how he has no job, has no car, lives in his sister's basement, barely has clothes or shoes and how he drinks alcohol on a daily basis now. He called himself an alcoholic. This is something I have asked him to confess to for months. Gerald even went on to mention how he has dark thoughts about himself. He talked about how he hates that he is overweight. I personally do not believe he has gained excessive weight, but I know it is an insecurity he has.

Gerald then stated how he hates how his facial appearance is. I have always noticed that this was a insecurity of his.

I told Gerald for months to go to therapy for his low self-esteem issues.

I suffer with low self-esteem also. I told him we could both go to therapy or go separately.

Gerald then started discussing the importance of building a relationship with God and how he needs to start to build one on his own. I knew this was Gerald's way of calming me down because Gerald knows how sensitive I am when God is involved in our conversations. So, I began to encourage him. I told Gerald to take a picture of his bedroom. Gerald sent the picture by text.

In the picture, Gerald had junk everywhere. A person would not be able to enter his room, due to how cluttered it was. I said to him, "Gerald, this picture is the life you live. You are everywhere at once. You are dysfunctional. Stop talking about your problems and fix them. Stop letting your problems become cluttered in your mind. God will help you clean up your life, but the choice is always up to you to fix your life. You make the choice. Take a notebook and start out by writing down your thoughts, feelings, goals, etc. Watch how God will enter into your heart, just by simply releasing your feelings." Gerald responded, saying, "Eb I talk to God every day." I responded, "Can you not see that God is saying, that is not enough! If all you did was talk to me on the phone in our relationship, it would not last. Your efforts of scheduling time to see me consistently, willingly spending money on me, planning out our date nights, experiencing intimacy, that's what made our relationship last. Communication is key in any relationship, but it's not enough to stand alone. God feels the same way in the relationship we build with him. God will always take care of us, but if you are still not satisfied and you state that you pray often, you are having a one-sided conversation. You are doing a lot of the talking, but are you listening to God after you pray? God is always telling us what he wants from us, when we tell him what we want from him. God will make us stay exactly where we do not want to be until he gets our undivided attention. It is just like in school. If all the students were talking when they should have not been, the teacher would say, "I'll wait" or sometimes make us miss recess. Recess is most students' favorite part of the day. All because students were talking over the teacher and she could not get everyone's attention, the students could not experience the best part of the day. Do not miss out on your blessings because you chose to stand in your own way. God's will, will always be done. If you think your life is going to go the direction you want, you are fooled. It is time to get activated in the kingdom!"

I do not think people understand that it is in your lowest place, when God will show up and out for you. I am not referring to money, a dream job or an extravagant car. I am referring to God's strength, peace, favor, love, grace, mercy, and his joy. Things money cannot buy! Some of you may say, "Well that's nice and all, but I prefer the money, the dream job or a fancy car." It's the people that get too consumed in money, that try to buy their own definition of peace, love, joy, etc. These people buy it through alcohol and sex. People want to feel what God could give us instantly in their own way! These people fail to realize their way is only a temporary fix. It will always do more damage than good, ultimately in the end.

When you suffer in your lowest place in life, only depending on God to help you get through, God will always give you access to his strength, peace, favor, love, grace, mercy, and his joy. These gifts God gives are not a temporary fix, but a permanent fix. When you let your light shine through Jesus Christ, everyone will see how strong, confident and loving you are. It may intimidate others, but they are not going to know how God brought you out of a dark place. They will not know how God helped you from not taking your own life, because life will make you want to do it. Let me tell you some of my story.

At the age of nine, I was sexually assaulted by my late great grandmother's late husband. Whenever I came over to my great grandmother's house, he was always friendly. I always had to go to my great grandmother's house as a child because my mom was a single mother. Unfortunately, my mom did not have much help and could not afford babysitters.

I, absolutely, could not stand going over to my great grandmother's house. My preference was always to go over to my late grandfather's house. He would spoil me rotten. He would take me to buy toys, buy me a bunch of goodies, take me to the playground, and much more. My great grandmother did none of these things. Instead, I was always stuck sitting at the dinner table, watching a series of Divorce Court with her, while she chatted on the telephone with her homegirls.

My great grandmother would force me to take naps throughout the day and read books. She also was extremely strict. I could barely utter a word, without her telling me I'm being disrespectful. Being at my great grandmother's house felt like a children's prison.

So, when she announced she was getting married, I had hoped he could be anything better than how she was.

Surprisingly, he was!

Her new husband would play card games, draw pictures with crayons, play hand games, and solve puzzles with me. When he came around, my great grandmother's house no longer felt like a children's prison, it was a children's playroom.

Until one day, it was no longer a children's playroom.

My great grandmother's home was no longer a children's prison either, it was actually worse.

On this particular day, my great grandmother and her new husband sat in the kitchen, watching tv shows.

My grandmother was reading her newspapers and chatting on the phone.

I walked over to play hand games with her husband.

My great grandmother had her back turned to us, still talking on the phone.

My great grandmother's husband and I were laughing from having fun. It was hilarious because I kept losing.

Suddenly, he tickled me and I laughed even harder. While he was tickling me, he proceeded to touch me inappropriately from the waist down.

My mom taught me at an early age about my body parts, so I knew this was wrong.

I grabbed his hand and immediately pushed him off of me.

I played it off with a laugh out loud because honestly, I was scared.

My great grandmother yelled to me, "Be quiet girl, can you not see that I am on the phone?"

I walked over to where my great grandmother was sitting and placed my chair right in front of her and did not look his way.

After that day, I hoped that I did not have to return back to my great grandmother's house. Although, I knew my mom needed me to go over to her house, since my mom had no help.

During this time, my mom's mother, my grandmother, was hospitalized with colon cancer. My grandmother was not doing well, in fact, she was dying. My mom was the only sibling out of her three siblings that took full responsibility for being there for their mom. So, I did not want to tell my mom what my great grandmother's husband had done to me.

I went back to my great grandmother's house a couple days later, after her husband had touched me inappropriately. On this day, my great grandmother needed to go to the post office across the street.

Usually when we had to go make a quick run, she would have me washing in the bathtub and getting dressed, even if we only went to the grocery store. So, I guess, because it was only across the street, she told me that I would be ok. Since the post office was across the street and she was going there quickly.

I told her I should be fine.

My great grandmother reassured me she would be back within at least five to ten minutes.

My gut had told me something suspicious was up. I should have trusted my intuition and went with my grandmother to that post office.

When my grandmother left, I heard her husband walking fast throughout the house.

I sat in the kitchen, praying he did not do anything to me.

What was strange is, when my grandmother is there, he always walks slowly, stating that his back hurts. He even walks around the house with a walker. He was eighty-seven at the time, so it was normal, but not today.

Today, however, he walked back and forth like a young teenaged man. He was pacing and I was scared.

Seconds later, he rushed and grabbed me.

He began kissing my lips.

He then proceeded by slowly taking off all of my clothes and trying to molest me.

My body went into shock, while he did these disgusting things to me. I could not move. I remember tears rolling down my face.

As he now unbuckled his pants, I knew I had to find where my body went and snap out of the shock I was in. I tapped into my inner strength and pushed him off of me. I screamed at him and said, "Get your hands off of me!"

After I had pushed him off, my great grandmother rang the doorbell.

She must have locked herself out or forgot her key. It did not matter, I was just happy she returned back! I hurried to put my clothes on and wiped away my tears so my grandmother would not notice anything peculiar. Before I could open the door for her, her husband beat me to it. I guess he did not want me to tell her what happened.

Soon as my great grandmother walked in, she looked at me, with a frown and said, "Why would you make him get up and answer the door? You could've picked your little legs up to open the door for me!" I responded, "I'm sorry".

Then she kissed her husband, walked into the kitchen and he went upstairs.

After this day, I kept this secret to myself.

A couple weeks later, my grandmother, my mom's mother, who was also my great grandmother's daughter, passed away. She died from surgery complications. My mom was beyond distraught and so was my great grandmother. Now, all my mom had was my great grandmother, for support. To make my great grandmother and my mom deal with this situation of me being sexually assaulted, would be selfish of me. Especially, at such a sensitive time, as this. So, I could not tell my mom or great grandmother what had happened.

Almost three months had passed and I still had not told my mom about how my great grandmother's husband sexually assaulted me. Almost every single night since I had experienced my great grandmother's husband touching me, taunted me in my sleep. His face would always appear, when I closed my eyes to go to bed, causing me to become sleep deprived from fear. The level of fear I had increased each day, making me feel as if every man in this world was out to get me! I felt uncomfortable being around my own father. To keep such a traumatic experience, as a secret, felt like I was putting myself in a pot full of misery. I knew that eventually, I had to tell my mom what happened, or else, I would lose my sanity. So, one night, I had to overcome my fear. It was time to tell my mom what happened.

During this time, my mom and I lived in a one-bedroom apartment. We both had twin beds in our room.

While my mom was sleeping at midnight, I sat up, and asked my mom, with a timid tone, if she could wake up. My mom said, "Yes, what's wrong?"

Fear arose back into my mind again and I struggled to say what was going on.

I began to stutter.

Then I began to cry.

This made my mom quickly get up out of bed, with deep concern.

My mom sat up on her bed and cleared her throat. She then followed and said, "Ebony, what is going on?"

I responded, "Mom, whatever you do, please do not get upset." I could tell the fear I had in me, trickled over to her. Immediately her eyes grew wide and she responded, "Ok, I will not get mad. What is it?"

I said, "Mom, do you promise?" She said, "Yes, I promise."

Although I was nervous to indulge into this secret that I have kept for months now, I believed my mom when she promised to remain calm. I felt safe and the fear I had slowly disappeared.

I proceeded to tell her every detail of what my great grandmother's husband put me through. I even went into how I could not sleep at night due to the trauma of being sexually assaulted.

I never knew there would be healing in confessing a secret so deep to my mom.

Children, teenagers, and even adults hide so many things from their parents, such as situations like this, due to how they feel their parents would react. The integrity of my mom keeping her promise, allowed her to become closer than a mother to me in that moment. She became my mother and my best friend.

Now, the healing that I am referring to, was not being healed from being sexually assaulted. The healing came from the release of hiding secrets. Keeping dark secrets can make people lose their mind. I believe it is the root cause of dementia.

Nevertheless, my mom hugged me and told me, "You are going to be alright, I will handle it." I cried while I hugged her, but I felt a lot better.

A couple days later from that night, I asked my mom if she had handled the situation. My mom told me that she had called my great grandmother. She told my great grandmother what had occurred when she left for the post office that day, between her husband and I.

Due to the security my mom gave me on handling the situation, I was happy to know my great grandmother finally knew. The assurance my mom gave me, made me know that my great grandmother was definitely going to punish him and leave him.

I wished someone could've told me that I was going to be wrong.

I was fooled.

In fact, it did not result in my favor, it was actually the opposite.

My mom said on the call, my great grandmother responded, "My husband is saying he did not do those things and that Ebony is lying." My mom then said, "Come on mom-mom, you and I both know Ebony would not lie about anything like this! He did it! I saw my daughter's face and the tears in her eyes! He tried to rape my daughter! How could you not believe her?"

My great grandmother gets quiet and takes a deep breath. She told her husband in the background, to calm down and that she knew me to know, I was not lying. Her husband tried telling my grandmother that he loves her and not to believe me.

My mom went on to finish this conversation by saying, she overheard my great grandmother talking to him in the background, telling her husband how that type of stuff is unacceptable. Her husband apologized to her and they both hung up. That was it.

Can you all believe after this conversation, my mom still sent me back over there? I did not have fear anymore. Instead, I was angry.

I never would have thought that this anger would stay in my heart, until I became an adult. Anger that I did not know, would later cause anger issues for me. Anger that I did not know, would cause emotional damage, that would ultimately affect my relationships.

When I had returned to my great grandmother's house, she seemed to act as if nothing had ever happened. I could not stand to be around her or her husband.

I sat in the kitchen with my great grandmother, while she cooked dinner. In walks, her no good husband, smiling. I rolled my eyes at him and did not utter a single word. My great grandmother looks at me and says, "Do you not see anyone else in the room? You better speak before you get in trouble!" Taking a deep breath, I said, "Hello!", with a fake five second grin. He responds, "Hey, how are you!" I shook my head with disgust and looked at the television.

How can people sit front row center at your pain and act as if they had seen nothing! My great grandmother could care less about how I felt and that truly hurt!

My grandmother went to the bathroom upstairs and her husband went to lay down on the couch in the living room.

I stayed in the kitchen.

Before my great grandmother left, she had set each one of our plates of food at the dinner table, so we could eat, once she had come back from the bathroom.

I took advantage of the opportunity of being alone in the kitchen, to figure out how I could hurt her husband.

I touched the knives in the kitchen drawer, contemplating how I should hurt him. Then I thought, I cannot do that. I cannot afford to go to prison. I told myself I had to harm him in a way that's unnoticeable.

So, I took a sharpie marker and drew all over his food.

I felt so good inside knowing I took matters into my own hands! This man needed to feel the pain that I was experiencing!

The question is, why can't things just go my way?

Then boom! My great grandmother caught me! A part of me wanted to cry, but the other part of me could care less, just like her. I guess I wanted to cry because evil was not in my heart. I was a good child. I was just filled with hurt.

She told me, "I caught you! You should be punished, but I am going to let your mother do it!" When my mom picked me up in her car, I was nervous that I would get in trouble, but I knew my truth would save me. As my mom drove, she remained quiet. About ten minutes later, she said, "Why did you color mom mom's husband's food with a sharpie?" I responded, "Because, I was angry." She looks at me and says, "I understand and I am not mad at you for doing what you did. You are not in trouble. Actually, you will not be going over mom mom's house for a while." After that day, I stopped going over there, for a long while. Unless my mom and I had visited her.

Eventually, when I grew older, I could go over to my great grandmother's house alone and still speak to her and her husband. I still disliked what she allowed me to suffer with, but I learned to push past my pain.

I longed for an apology from her. Years went by, my grandmother was now in her eighties. I told myself, one day she would acknowledge her wrongs and then I can heal from my hurt. I always thought she would live until she was a hundred years old, so I knew as the years progressed, we would talk about what I endured. Again, I was wrong. The older I became, she developed dementia. She remembered my face, but she barely remembered my name. Although I knew she was forgetting all of her memories, I had hoped that she would remember what I suffered with and still talk about it with me. So that I can be healed and set free. In December of 2020, she died.

It's unfortunate that my grandmother died, never apologizing to me for her husband sexually assaulting me. She at least could have apologized for still staying with him, while she knew what her husband had done to me. All I wanted was some accountability for the pain I endured, but I never received an apology.

The following year, her husband died.

Neither one of them ever acknowledged my hurt. Neither one of them showed remorse. All the trauma they both have caused me, including the fear I had of men and the anger, I now had to find a way to heal on my own.

Sometimes, people will die, never acknowledging the damage they have caused to your life. I longed for an apology, almost my whole life, not knowing, I never needed it. I allowed the anger built in me as a child, to cause mess in my future.

Forgiveness is necessary. If you do not forgive, you will always suffer. Even if you are not suffering at this moment, you will suffer. Forgive now, so you can heal better from your future traumatic experiences, because there are blessings in suffering. We just make the choice to miss it, when we choose the enemy's way, instead of God's way.

I wished I grabbed that concept earlier in life because the anger I kept internally, made my other life situations I went through later in life, worse. Really, it's why I could not last in any of my relationships.

Who would have thought I would have become a young mother, seven years after being sexually assaulted? I never pictured myself being sixteen and pregnant, but it happened.

My pregnancy was one of the hardest things I went through in my life! I fell in love with a man that finally made me feel safe around men. Not knowing that, he would control every man around me, or impregnate me with a little man. Initially I was supposed to get an abortion, but God made me choose not to. If you are wondering why I was going to choose to get an abortion, it was because my child's father trapped me! Yes, trapped me! It is a real thing and my child's father admitted to it. Now, I know it takes two to tango, but this was not what happened.

My mom warned me that it would happen with the first pregnancy scare I had. She told me the lord told her because my child's father did not want any other man to have me. Again, my child's father was very controlling.

God is not a man that should lie and he will always send warning before destruction.

What I did not know however, is destruction is how God connects you back to his promise.

Although battling between choosing an abortion or keeping a child was a hard decision to make, it was the first time I had heard from God. My walk with God had changed for the better.

The day before the abortion surgery, God told me, "Do not do it! I know you feel like this is not fair. This is a lot to handle, but know that I will bless you and your son. I will make sure you and your son will have everything you both need. Be obedient to my will and I will ensure blessings for as long as you shall live!"

My mom has always taught me that obedience is better than sacrifice. So, I chose at that moment, to be obedient to God.

After I made that decision, when I went to church that following Sunday, my Bishop had prayed for me. He said to me "Ebony, God said, you and your son will not want for anything. God is going to make this journey easy for you. He is going to make sure you and your son are beyond blessed!"

Instantly, I knew how real God was.

All the tears, pain and depression, was meaningful because I was able to hear from God. I was able to understand his will for my life.

Once I was able to not live for others, I was able to understand my assignment on earth.

When I had my son, I walked with God, with my head low, at first. I never saw myself becoming a baby mom, let alone a single baby mom. A baby mom fighting to graduate high school. A baby mom fighting for a minimum wage job. The worst fight of them all, a baby mom fighting for her child's father to want to be active and present in our child's life. This could not be God's will. This could not be what god promised me, it just cannot be.

Money was so low, that I had to buy clothes from the thrift store.

Jobs were not working out for my mom either.

My mom suffered from foot issues at the time and had her car repossessed. Now I was forced to carry my son on public transportation.

My step mom started struggling with jobs as well, during this time.

To make matters worse, my child's father's family disliked me. Why? There was no specific reason at all. They always ganged up on me. They bullied me and even tried to fight me on many occasions.

My family neglected me.

I could only rely on my mom and my step mom.

People at my church treated me differently, assuming I did secular things outside of church. I heard rumors that I was the average pregnant "young one", whatever that meant.

My friends stopped talking to me.

I was living a nightmare.

To experience church hurt and family hurt all at once, can feel as if someone has stabbed you in the heart and in the back. I had to bled out alone.

When I had reached twelfth grade, my school dean told me the only way that I would graduate high school would be if I completed eight classes with two added elective classes. I had perseverance, however it felt impossible to achieve. With determination, I graduated, but it did not take away from the pain I felt.

Still, years later, the pain cuts deeper and deeper. I felt as if I needed acceptance from the world. I needed to prove why I was not an average baby mom. I figured the best way to prove this was by forcing my child father to be a family with our son. I fought to keep our family. I accepted my child's father controlling me, cheating on me, and manipulating me just to keep our family. In my young mind, I always thought no man wants a young single woman with a child. So, I had to stay. No one was going to love or accept me.

Eventually, I did leave my child's father, with hopes that another man would love me, but I was fooled. I experienced so many men manipulating me and using me. All of them were just pitiful men. After a while, I had to learn to fall in love with myself and not seek acceptance from others. The moment I did, God gave me Gerald.

Ladies, the man that is meant for you, will always be standing right in front of you, once you stop searching for one.

Gerald and I have been friends for years. Actually, correction, we were best friends for years. We would call each other almost every other day, talking for hours. Gerald and I always laughed until we cried. We would go out to eat at restaurants, go to the mall, and go to the movies. As much time we spent together, I never looked at him as a person of romantic interest. People would always say, "Gerald has a crush on you, but I did not believe it." I never understood, why can't a female and a male just be friends? It seems to be a hard thing. At least, it's what I truly wanted. Especially knowing Gerald cared about me. A man does not have to be your boyfriend to love you.

Sad reality is, a man is a man and if he's showing all of these characteristics, that man does in fact, like you. That man might even love you and in this instance, Gerald, indeed, loved me.

The moment Gerald and I kissed, I knew he was the one for me. My intuition told me. I just felt it. The feeling was unexplainable. Then I prayed about what I had felt and God sent confirmation to me.

It's important to know, however, God can send confirmation, but your life situation will often appear as the opposite of what God said.

When I told Gerald, we should be together, he ran from me immediately. Gerald blatantly flirted with other females in front of me. He even asked me to just be his friend with benefits. Gerald had told me that he did not see himself ever being in a relationship with anyone.

Fun fact, no one can run from what God has already ordained. If God spoke it, it shall come to pass! Run all you want. Eventually, what you are running from, will catch you!

Days, weeks and months had gone past. I watched Gerald run. As he ran from the relationship, it did hurt. It hurt so bad, we had several occasions, that I had to end our friendship. I would block him, but we always managed to still talk within the following week. By the next week, Gerald and I would be hanging out somewhere again. Honestly, this cycle brought us closer, than it did apart.

My friends would put in my ear, Gerald was using me for his own benefit or he does not like you the way you like him. However, my friends did not know what God told me. They could not understand why I could look past the rejection.

Within the next couple of months, Gerald told me how he was in love with me, but was afraid. He came to my doorstep asking me to be with him. I learned even more, how real God is. I learned how to trust in God, even when my situation is not going the direction I want it to go in. You never know when your "It came to pass" moment will come.

Now I know you are thinking, how did you end up here, with Gerald now? Sometimes when you are too focused on the promises God has shown you, you lose sight of how God is shaping, molding and changing you to be ready to receive his promise to you. We get consumed in our own happiness, that we stand in our way of receiving what God desires for us to have. Somewhere down the line, in Gerald's and I relationship, I did just that.

I never stopped praying. I never stopped believing. I never stopped building a relationship with God, but I started building my relationship my way and not the way God intended.

I prayed each and every day that God would create me into a virtuous woman so Gerald and I would be married. I had to pray that prayer because God told me in the beginning of dating Gerald, that we would be married. So, in order to get to his promise, I needed to become a woman worth marrying. At least, that's what I assumed. I wanted the Lord to make me a wife Gerald would want to come home to. With asking these things, however, I still chose to live my life, the way I wanted to. I allowed the enemy to control me, more than God because I blocked out God's will.

My anger was something the enemy took advantage of, since I was sexually assaulted. All because I choose not to be healed. Not only did this create a monster in me, but this monster crawled into Gerald. Sporadically, we were unhappy with one another, but loved each other deeply.

Where I am, today with my life, I truly want God to change me from the inside out. I want God to create in me a new heart, mind, body and pure spirit. I just have to always aim to see the bigger picture. I have to aim to see the future outcome and not the present. Most importantly, I have to aim to forgive, in order to be fully healed from my past trauma.

I guess my only question now is, what is the picture that God wants me to see?

God says, "Practice getting out of your emotions and trusting my will. Practice forgiveness. Lastly, practice to be obedient. No matter what your life may appear to be, if I said it, regardless of what the devil meant for evil, it must come to pass, for your good!"

Sincerely,
Back to trusting God

Chapter 9

THE FIGHT FOR STRENGTH

DAY 9

Dear Diary, *December 25th, 2022*

Trusting his will is hard.

I could barely sleep last night. I did not cry, but I was in a depressed state of mind. No one wants to celebrate the holidays, miserable. Well, at least I did not.

Despite how I felt, I pushed myself to enjoy Christmas. I have a lot to be thankful for and watching my son open his gifts I bought him, is the best part. I told myself that today will be a great day, on purpose. I choose happiness. When I affirmed my joy, it turned out to be a beautiful day.

My son loved every gift I bought him. I bought him a new phone, clothes, shoes and more. My mom bought me Loui Vuitton earrings I had been asking her for months. I was ecstatic. My stepmom had bought me a pair of sneakers I have been begging her for also. It was truly a beautiful morning.

Church was one of the best parts of my day also. My church family are the most caring, genuine individuals that you could ever meet. Gerald's family also attends my church, so at first it was challenging, not thinking about Gerald. However, Gerald's family are beyond sweet and they do not make anything awkward. So, this made it easier to push through my challenges.

As I listened to the sermon today, my pastor mentioned that the greatest things in our lives are birthed at the most inconvenient times for us. This statement was so profound, on so many levels. It sent chills throughout my body. I needed to hear it, especially in this season of my life.

Remember, God is not allowing you to birth your promises when you feel or look good. During this sermon, while my pastor preached, God started speaking to me. God said, "It is not about you birthing a greater relationship with Gerald. It is not about the next chapter in your relationship. It is about the birth of the new Ebony." I told God, "I will remove myself and I chose you to change me."

After church, I went to my mom's house. My entire family was there and were ready to feast. When I saw my family, once I had entered my mother's home, I went upstairs to calm my emotions down. I was always used to Gerald and I, spending the holidays with one another. So seeing my family happy, just made me emotional again.

I went into my son's bedroom, upstairs. I cried and told myself that it was time to push past my pain, again. After I wiped my tears, I told God to speak to me. I needed him to say something to me, something that would give me strength to push through. God remained silent, which told me he was up to something. Also know that, when God is silent, he is either working harder for something you need or speaking louder than you think.

So, I went back downstairs. I had an amazing time, laughing, cooking and talking with my family. It's always refreshing when you can push past your pain internally and smile externally. It identifies strength. I knew I was stronger and it made me proud of myself.

As the night came to an end, I checked Gerald's Instagram page. Gerald did not post anything on his page. This told me that today was also a difficult day for Gerald. So, I knew I had to head home.

Why was this day so hard? I have no answers, but I pushed through it all. I am happy I did.

Sincerely,
Pushing Strength

Chapter 10

ONLY TRUST GOD

DAY 10

Dear Diary,   *December 26, 2022*

I woke up today, feeling awkward.

I had too many mixed emotions.

A part of me felt happy to know how strong I truly was. The other part of me knew Gerald still loved me. I knew we both wanted our relationship to work itself out.

Now, I remember God told me that I had to go through this alone, yet I was still searching for answers, through someone else. I needed to vent to someone other than God, but I fail to understand that, obedience is better than sacrifice.

Who else better to talk to, then my mother?

I went to go find my mom. She was in her office.

I asked for her opinion on Gerald. She stated, "I know that Gerald loves you, but he only wants to love you on his terms. Gerald wants to be with you, while he has relations with multiple women. Gerald is not ever going to let you go. He's probably going to persuade you to be his main lady, while he keeps the other women around."

As I listened to my mom's unintentional discouragement, I could not help thinking that I should have stayed silent. God told me to only talk to him in this season in my life and I sacrificed to do what I wanted. It was not worth sacrificing for. Now I'm emotional, all over again.

Nevertheless, I could not stay miserable today because I had promised my son that I would take him to the mall. I wanted my son and I to have a fun-filled day. So, my son and I left and enjoyed our day together. We had such a great day, that I totally forgot about my situation with Gerald. Retail therapy is so essential. It helps to clear your mind.

Once I came home, I checked my laptop, to see if Gerald reached out, since I had him blocked on my phone. This is the beauty of having Apple software products. My intuition was right. Gerald had messaged me multiple times, telling me that he loves me. Gerald reached out on Christmas Eve and Christmas Day, apologizing. As much as I wanted to reach out, I knew Gerald knew that I had him blocked. I was nervous and ashamed of myself, so I did not reach back out to him. Until I went on social media.

At this moment I am not supposed to go on social media, since I am on my own love fast.

So, when I slipped up and went to go on social media anyway, I was so upset with myself. I dislike making promises to God that I cannot keep. God never fails me, yet, I often fail him. God always provides for me and told me in his word, I have not because I ask not. Yet, here I am, asking God for a reward that money cannot buy. God told me obedience is better than sacrifice, yet I continue to be disobedient and sacrifice being on social media.

Later that night, I went on Gerald's social media page, to see what he was up to.

As soon as I hacked his page, I opened his direct messages. In Gerald's direct messages, were different females he had flirted with.

Before I could react with my emotions, I threw my phone across the room and told God how I felt. I told God to forget about all of this. My prayers, fasting, obedience, made me feel as if I am following God's will, yet God allowed me to get hurt by this man, again and again and again. How much more is God going to put me through? I am tired. I QUIT! I do not care what God has for me! If this is what the devil called winning, then fine, he has won! My heart cannot take any more pain.

After I let out these frustrations, I cried for hours. I cried abruptly. My tears would not stop. I had no one to call on.

It's unbelievable how when you are in your lowest moments in life, all you have left is to call on God.

You sit there, wondering, is God even listening? Is God here?

In these moments, he will seem as if he's so quiet. It will feel as if God does not exist, but honestly, that's when he is talking to you, the most. It is just harder to interpret what God is saying, when we stand in our own way.

It's like asking someone a question, but each time they answer the question, you put your headphones on and tune them out. How are you ever going to listen, with so many distractions playing loudly?

After crying for almost two and a half hours, it clicked to me, suddenly. I did express to Gerald my frustrations, again, on my computer though. After being frustrated with Gerald, I blocked him because I knew I had to talk to God without being distracted.

While I sat on my bed, wiping away my tears, God had revealed so much, at once. I know in the chapters prior, I gave a few details of Gerald's and I relationship, however, it's time to tell what really happened. Let me give you all the backdrop of Gerald's and I story.

So, here it is.

As I told you all before, Gerald and I started off as close friends. We truly loved each other. Whenever I had a fun girl's night out, Gerald was the only person I could rely on to get me home safely. I knew I could call Gerald anytime, anyplace and he would always show up. Gerald was so supportive of me and I was the same way for him. Especially, when Gerald's mom had died and surprisingly, that's when our romance began.

When Gerald called me, notifying that his mother was rushed to ICU, I told him I would come to the hospital immediately. I came to the hospital at one o'clock in the morning, with my mother. When I entered the room, the doctors had Gerald and his siblings waiting for results. Gerald's face lit up when he saw me enter the waiting room.

Gerald's mom was on a life machine and the doctors informed his family that more than likely she was not going to live. So, my mom and I prayed with his family and talked with them for hours, to keep them in great spirits.

Until Gerald and his siblings started to break down, emotionally. We were all talking about great memories about his mother and when his siblings asked Gerald about a memory, he could not hold back his tears any much longer. Gerald yelled, "This is all not fair!" and punched a hole into the wall, with his fist. After he had punched the wall, he ran out of the room and slammed the door. No one reacted upset with Gerald, because we understood how he felt. My mom whispered to me, "Ebony, go out there and check on him!" I walked out the room and ran over to Gerald. He fell on the floor crying. I did not know what to say, I just wanted him to release his emotions.

So, I helped him off the floor, and let him lay down on my lap, while he cried so hard.

He was distraught.

I was teary eyed, seeing him so hurt. I wished it did not have to be this way. I could not imagine losing my mom, but I have lost a close loved one before.

I remember crying at my job, when I found out they passed away so I knew how Gerald felt, in a way, but I'm sure the pain he felt during this moment was worse.

All I could do was rub Gerald's back, while he cried, letting him know I will always be here.

Gerald's best friend came out of the room to sit with us and made Gerald feel better. His best friend cracked a couple of jokes and Gerald started laughing again.

Gerald, his best friend, and I went back into the waiting room and went back to talking about great memories.

Gerald and I sat next to each other and held hands.

Once I told him I had to leave, I could tell he was sad, again.

When my mom and I had left the waiting room, my mom said to me, "You know after being there for Gerald, he is going to have love for you, forever. It is in times like this, when people realize who's meant for them." I responded to my mom, "Gerald knows that I will always have his back, like I would with any of my friends." My mom then responded, "Yeah I know, but this time it is different."

I ignored my mom because I knew what she was implying, but I only viewed Gerald as a close friend.

Every day, after that night, I called Gerald to check on him and his mental state. I would take Gerald to the movies, out to restaurants, to the arcade, and he would even spend the night on my couch. I was truly there for him in every capacity.

The week following, was his mother's memorial ceremony. Gerald's family rented out a banquet hall to celebrate her life. It was a beautiful ceremony. Gerald's family had so much delicious food. They also had a DJ come play music. All of Gerald's family was on the dance floor, grooving. Each one of Gerald's siblings gave an amazing tribute. It was truly the best way to send their mom off to heaven.

At the end of the ceremony, Gerald's family released doves into the air. This was sentimental to Gerald and his siblings. All of Gerald's family began to get emotional, while the music played and the birds flew up into the sky. I walked over to Gerald, hugged him tightly, and whispered into his ear, "I will always have your back, for life!" He responded, "I know. I will have yours, also." After the release of the doves, my mom and I left the ceremony.

As my mom and I got into her car, my mom said to me, "I am telling you Ebony, after seeing how Gerald's face lit up again when you came to his mother's memorial ceremony, I promise you, Gerald is going to cherish you forever!" I told her, "You're probably right mom." We jiggled and my mom drove off.

A couple of days later, Gerald and I went to the mall. Then Gerald and I went back to my house to watch movies. When I started getting tired, I walked into my room to go to bed. While I walked towards my room, Gerald yelled, "Ebbuwebb, come back out here and sleep on the couch with me." I told Gerald, "Boy, bye. What do I look like?" He laughed and responded, "No, silly. I am just a little scared. Could you sleep on the opposite end of the couch?" Instantly, I thought, he definitely just lost his mom and it's probably a lot to handle right now. So, I said, with a big smile, "Ok, fine." I told Gerald to make sure he slept on the opposite end.

Gerald and I watched movies until we fell asleep that night. After that night, Gerald still would come over to my house to spend the night, but he knew to sleep on the couch. I loved how he respected that rule and did not take advantage of it, at least I thought.

One night, Gerald came over to my house and asked me to lay on the couch with him, again. He then asked me to hold his hand. I responded, "Um, ok.", although it felt strange. Gerald said to me, "If our hands fall apart, place your legs on top of mine, so I can feel you near, while I sleep." I simply just shook my head, in agreement.

Slowly, he started to rub my body, smoothly, while still laying on the opposite side of the couch. Of course, I allowed it. I was trying to play along, with whatever Gerald had up his sleeve. I also knew Gerald was vulnerable, so I did not want to make anything between us awkward.

As soon as I closed my eyes, trying to ignore Gerald's gentle hands, rubbing up on my leg, Gerald yanks me from the end of my shirt and kisses me. It was not a simple kiss, we started passionately, kissing.

My heart was racing and so was his. I was not sure if it was right. Kissing my best friend, while he just lost his mom, could sound odd, but somehow, I felt as if I was in a fairytale. This was a romantic fairytale, whose story will last forever. The sparks of love filled my living room. The way we kissed, felt as if we had always wanted to. It was like our hearts finally received what it had been longing for.

After passionately kissing Gerald, for about five long minutes, I pushed him away. I told him, "Gerald, we cannot do this. This is not right or maybe it is, it's just the wrong timing." Gerald looked deep into my eyes and said, "Ebony, just come here." We began kissing, once more.

Gradually, we began taking our clothes off, to get intimate. He laid me down and proceeded to get intimate. Before we initiated intimacy, I looked Gerald into his eyes and said, "I love you." Immediately, he responded, "Really?" I shook my head and said, "Yes, really." I could tell Gerald knew I was serious. I told him this because I know how men are, whether he was my best friend or not. I knew if Gerald really loved me or cared for me, he would not just become intimate with me just to let off stress. If Gerald reveals the truth, I will not feel used or emotionally attached.

Men will play manipulative tricks to ultimately get what they want sometimes. Men view women as a game of chess, not realizing the queens make all the moves on the board. The queen is the most powerful player in chess, yet you need a king on the board, usually to win a checkmate. If you learn the concept of chess well, you will know how to beat these men at their own game of chess.

Gerald then stood up and placed his clothes back on. He said, "Let's just go to sleep." Instantly, I knew that he cared about me.

I cannot lie, after that night, it was awkward being around Gerald. We tried our best to pretend as if nothing had ever happened.

Until, a few days later, the awkwardness between Gerald and I changed.

I invited Gerald to go with my mom and I out to eat, for my mom's birthday. Gerald told me he was busy, but surprised me, by showing up anyway.

My mom, her friends, Gerald and I had an amazing time at dinner. We enjoyed ourselves so much, that after Gerald and I left the restaurant and went back to my home, to spend quality time with one another,

Once Gerald and I had arrived back home, we watched movies and cuddled.

Cuddling eventually led to us kissing again, but this time, I told Gerald, "What are you doing? What are you doing?" Gerald responded saying, "Ebbuwebb, we are just rocking this out". I told Gerald after his response, "Well if you want to kiss me, cuddle with me, and send mixed signals, this is not rocking out, this is a relationship." Gerald said to me, "Ok, forget it, I'll stop making you feel uncomfortable."

Of course, you all know, men always aim for what it is they really want to get from women. If anything, men will continue to play the game of chess, waiting to see what's your next move, so that they can tempt you and conqueror. Gerald had conquered his game.

After we had discussed our intentions with one another, we started kissing again.

I would like to say Gerald could not control himself around me, but the truth is, I could not control myself around him. Maybe, I had these feelings for Gerald all along, but never acknowledged them.

So, this time when Gerald slowly began to climb on top of me, I told him, "Remember what I said, if we move forward with this, it's not us rocking along, we will be in a relationship. I do not just become intimate with anyone." He told me, "Ok I understand." Then we made love or at least I hope it was love. I really had hoped so.

That following morning, as we cuddled on the couch, I turned over to look Gerald in his eyes. He immediately woke up and I asked him, "So, now are we officially together?" He looked at me with a smirk and said, "When did I ever agree to that?" I sat up, furious, and told him, "You literally agreed to it, before we were intimate!". He stared at me, while I began crying, with my veins almost bursting out of my head and said, "At this moment, I have different situations with other women and I do not know what status I am with them. So, I cannot commit to a relationship with you."

Gerald would have been better off, staying my friend, then using me in this magnitude.

I was so hurt.

How could Gerald be so hurtful? How?

I know you all are thinking, well, why could you still want to work things out now?

To answer that question, just follow along, the story changes dramatically.

All the hurt I felt, after hearing Gerald say those foul words to me, had led me to a sinking place. I went into the shower, after Gerald left that day and cried for hours. My heart did not want to believe Gerald was a user. Gerald was the last person that I had ever expected to hurt me.

Later, that day, I blocked Gerald for a month. Every single day of that month, I cried. My intuition had told me that Gerald would eventually come back around, but the pain I felt overwhelmed me. As the days grew, I started healing and the resentment towards Gerald began to fade away.

The next month, I started to miss him, just a little. Gerald was still my friend and I did not want to lose him. Due to my heart beginning to miss Gerald, I unblocked him, first, on my social media accounts. As soon as I unblocked Gerald on my social media accounts, he messaged me. His messages said, "I miss you so much and I love you Ebony. I just want my best friend back." The feeling was oh so mutual. I messaged Gerald back, saying, "I miss you also." He followed by saying, "I am going to call you later on today."

I waited by my phone all day. I could not wait to hear Gerald's voice. He called me around seven-thirty in the evening.. We laughed and caught each other up on what was going on in our lives, while we were not speaking. After about thirty minutes of talking on the phone with Gerald, he asked me to send him my location so he could pick me up. At the moment, I was at work. So, Gerald drove to my job and picked me up.

Gerald took me out to dinner, surprisingly.

After mingling at dinner with Gerald, we went back to my place to hang out. One thing led to another and we were back at square one, getting intimate again. To say how ashamed of myself I was, would be an understatement. I know Gerald told me he's not ready for a relationship, but somehow my heart tells me he is, but he's afraid.

The next morning, while Gerald and I laid, cuddling on the couch, Gerald told me that he wanted to start this romance thing between us, off slowly. Gerald was specific about going on dates, until we were really ready to be committed. Again, I responded, "Nope, if we are getting intimate with each other, then we are together", and again Gerald disagreed. Gerald did not want our disagreement to cause us to end our friendship again, but I could care less. So, I cut ties with Gerald, again. See, the thing about me is, I will go after what I want and in a odd way, I was chasing after him.

Instead of blocking Gerald, this time, I added him to my Instagram, close friends. For those that might be wondering, what are Instagram close friends? It is a small or large group that can be created by you, to only see private pictures or images of what you want your close friends to see. Not all of your followers on Instagram have access, just your close friends.

A tool my mom has always taught me is to always show people better than you can voice, that you are doing fine, with or without them.

Us females will tell men after a heartbreak, "Just wait until you see how the next man will treat me" or "I can always find someone new, there's plenty of fish in the sea!" In actuality, us females are not thinking of finding a new man and are probably lying in bed, crying over the same man who broke our heart.

So, on my close friends on Instagram, I would post myself, hanging out with other men. I would post captions such as, "Single life is so much fun, especially when you have options."

Every single post I made to my close friends on Instagram, Gerald was always the first viewer. I knew my plan was working.

About five posts later, from my Instagram close friends, Gerald finally reached out to me. He mentioned how he just wants to be friends. Around this time of the year, which was 2020, the world was suffering from the Covid-19 pandemic. So, everyone was forced to almost remain indoors.

During the beginning of the pandemic, when Gerald and I rekindled our friendship, he stayed at my home for a whole week.

My mom and stepmom loved every second of Gerald spending time at our home.

The four of us would watch movies, play board games, make Tik Tok videos, order food and more.

Gerald and I, still would get intimate with one another when everyone fell asleep.

By the fourth day of that week, I told Gerald that I believed we should be in a relationship. It was not because I wanted my way anymore, it was because God showed me that Gerald will be my husband in the future. I did not tell Gerald everything God had revealed to me because he was not as spiritual as me. So, I knew everything I was saying would be a bunch of nothing.

Gerald and I had a strong bond. The love is most certainly real. The friendship is genuine. If any one of you readers have already found your soulmate and you are happily married, then you know the unexplainable feeling of knowing that person was meant for you.

While I poured my heart out to Gerald, explaining still, how we should be in a relationship, I could tell Gerald was still not ready for commitment. Although I knew in my heart, he knew I was his soulmate. Right now, his battle is his heart and his mind. My problem was, I kept involving myself in a battle that was not mine to fight. Until Gerald could conquer his own battle, I would continue to get hurt each time I involved myself. Clearly, I was not using wisdom. Since, the love we had for one another was so strong, Gerald said, "Ok Ebbuwebb, we can be together, if that makes you happy." I asked him, "Gerald, do you honestly want to be in a relationship?" Gerald responded, "I honestly just want to date and gradually allow us to fall into a relationship, but I really care about how you feel. So, if this is what you want, then ultimately I will give it to you." I am going to pause the story here, to give some encouraging words of wisdom.

It does not matter how much God revealed to you, that someone is meant to be your significant other. It does not matter if you received confirmations, prophecies, visions, etc. Never force what God told you, because his timing is always different from ours. Especially, if an individual tells you that they are not ready, do not force them or persuade them.

God reveals so much to us about who is meant for us, but the main principle we can sometimes lack is that God will give both parties a choice. It does not matter whether the other party involved heard God say it, because everyone does not have the gift to hear from the holy spirit. However, that does not mean that God is not waiting on their answer. You may be ready, but you still have to wait.

If God does not force non-believers to believe in him, why should we force anything, on anyone? Now keep in mind, what God spoke to you, can feel as if it will never happen, especially if you do not go after it.

This is why following these steps will be important, so the process of waiting on your promise will not be rushed.

1. *Have patience (Patience is a virtue)* **Proverbs 25:15 (ERV)- With patience, you can make anyone change their thinking, even a ruler. Gentle speech is very powerful.**
2. *ALWAYS pray, everyday and as many times needed. (Prayer is essential because God will communicate with you how to have patience, each day, while you wait on what he promised you. It will give you hope, to believe that God will give what he promised you!)* **Luke 18:1 (ERV)- Then Jesus taught the followers that they should always pray and never lose hope.**
3. *Eliminate your plan (Your plan will NEVER work. Even if it seems like it is, I promise you it will not work. Follow God's plan. Ask God through prayer to align your plan with his will. Ask God to help you to follow his will each day, so that you do not get consumed in following your own plan. We all fall short of this rule, just remind yourself daily, not my will, but God's will be done)* **Jeremiah 29:11 (ERV)- I say this because I know the plans that I have for you. "This message is from the LORD." I have good plans for you. I don't plan to hurt you. I plan to give you hope and a good future.**

If we aim to follow these steps, consistently, we would be much further to having what God has promised us. A lot of times, it takes longer to receive what God has revealed because unfortunately, we stand in our own way.

Were we really listening to the song, God's plan or just simply, singing along to it?

We know God always has a plan for us, but does that really resonate in our minds?

Just as much as God has a plan for us, so does the enemy. The scripture says, in John 10 verse 10, *The thief's purpose is to steal and kill and destroy. My purpose is to give them a rich and satisfying life.*

Many of us Christians, are aware the devil has a plan, but we let the devil take charge of his plan, more than God's plan. It is unbelievable, right? We choose to consume alcohol, allowing spirits to take control of us. We follow social media trends, but do not follow Godly trends. Godly trends such as, attending church, giving our tithes and offerings, serving in God's house, forgiving others who have done us wrong, reading God's word, and more.

It's quite disturbing how individuals no longer like attending church because of it appearing as a religious cult or they do not like how leaders in the kingdom treat others.

The more individuals do not attend church, they lack spiritual feeding. When we attend church services, it's not about how we view our church, more than it is about making sure we receive the nutrients God has for us. It prepares us for the plans the enemy may have set up. It might not build up our immune system, like vitamins, but it builds up our spirit for any spiritual attacks we will endure.

I hope you all know whether you are a Christian or not, there will always be a spiritual attack coming to you. It is not meant to destroy you, more than it is meant to help build you. So, that you can help others, who are suffering in the kingdom.

Think about it, a weak man cannot help another weak man walk. Only a strong man can help to pick up a weak man and help him walk. God has the same concept. When we help others, by giving to the homeless, helping the sick, training others in sports, we feel good, once we see them accomplish. It's a benefitting feeling that lets you know that you contributed to changing that individual's life. Why is it we cannot allow God to help us win? Instead, these individuals who choose not to be spiritually fed, are being fed by the devil because we can only be fed by one or the other.

If you go into a boxing match, without being trained or prepared, you will lose the match. It may seem as though I am drifting off topic, but I am not.

I could have avoided a lot of the unnecessary hurt I went through with Gerald, had I removed my plan.

Chapter 13, in the book of Judges told us how the children of the Israelites had spent forty years oppressed. I truly believe had they not had been in their own way, they would have received their promise sooner. They were too stuck on the promise God had given to them, that they could not listen to what God was instructing them to do, while they waited.

My advice to anyone experiencing a similar situation as I did, is know that whatever God has told you, will happen because he promised it to you. Just walk with God and be obedient to his will, while you wait for the promise.

One of my favorite scriptures tells us, in the book Numbers 23 verse 19 that God is not a man, so he does not lie. He is not human, so he does not change his mind. Has he ever spoken and failed to act? Has he ever promised and not carried it through?

If God spoke it, then it has to happen! Even if it takes forty years, it will happen.

God never intends to make us wait longer for what he told us, was already ours, but if he does make us wait longer for our promise, then we have to align our plans with his will. Here's an example scenario:

> *You're a woman and you have finally heard from God, after always praying that you would hear his voice. One day, God speaks to you and tells you that you are about to receive a suburban five-bedroom house, with six bathrooms, a deck and even water. God even told you that you would own this home. God showed you an image of you flourishing in your life.*
>
> *Now what God had promised you was quite vague, but it had you excited. Until you remembered that your yearly salary is only twenty-five thousand dollars and you can barely afford your seven hundred dollar rent.*
>
> *Furthermore, your car breaks down every other week and you are raising two babies, one boy and one girl, on your own. You continuously remind yourself though, if God said it is mine, then it is mine!*

You wait around for about three weeks and still no house yet. So, you tell yourself, it is time to search for a higher paying job.

Thankfully, you receive a new job, two months later, at fifty-four thousand dollars a year, but you are still behind on your bills. Your car still keeps breaking down, children still need more clothes, food is hard to provide, you can never buy yourself anything nice, you feel financially drained.

It is now seven months later, you are still praying, reminding yourself of the promise God gave you of your brand-new house. That house was your dream and you continuously tell yourself, you will have it.

Since it is getting closer to the end of the year, you went back to college to finish your bachelor's degree in accounting, with hopes for a better salary. If you have a better salary, you will get the house God had told you about. You had not realized that registering back into classes would now require you to pay for after care for your children and hire babysitters.

You are still behind on your bills. Your car has now been repossessed and you have been evicted from your home. You are now living in a shelter with your two kids. You are still praying. You still have hope. You still attend church each Sunday, while also paying your tithes and offerings. Although your aim is to still please God, deep down inside, you feel like God has forgotten about you. It feels as if the promise God spoke, will never happen. No matter how much you push past how you feel, you are still struggling, stressed, overwhelmed and tired.

It's now two years later, after God spoke your promise to you, but yet your life looks the complete opposite of what God spoke. You are trying to hold on as best as you can to your promise, but it's only a short matter of time before you let it go.

Now you are drinking alcohol to remove stress. You are always at the bar or club on Saturday nights. You are always intoxicated, to relax your body. You even fornicate with people you barely know, to live again.

It is now four years later and your appearance has changed. You look how you feel. You have gained excessive weight, your lips are black from smoking often, you have bags under your eyes, you simply look emotionally drained. You had wished a man could come along by now to help ease the load, but you are still single. The party life is still fun on the weekends, but now you find yourself at the bar on weekdays. The party life helps you to not think about your daily problems. Especially since your brother was just recently murdered and he was your only reliable source of help. Now you really had to navigate life, feeling helpless.

Ten years later, after the promise God told you, and life has changed, for the better. You are now working two jobs, with an annual salary of seventy-thousand dollars. You also have a new clothing line that has bloomed. This apparel line has a following on social media of roughly fifth-teen thousand followers.

Since, your life has transformed, from following your own plan, you have tossed away your promise. You are still a Christian, but you do not attend church anymore for personal reasons. Mainly because while you attended church, none of the folks there were kind to you. Your friends you party on the weekend with though, are more reliable. They answered their phone more than the pastor would.

Six-teen years later, your kids have now graduated high school. Thankfully, both of your children went off to college. You are also newlywed. Your business is flourishing better than ever. Your husband does struggle with infidelity, sadly, but hey, life is amazing.

Your husband and you, have a three bedroom and two-bathroom home that you both are renting.

That promise God gave you, has been long forgotten.

You are satisfied with the house you have worked hard for. There is no need for a five-bedroom house in the suburbs anymore, especially since your children are off to college. You lost faith a long time ago. Life has thrown so many challenges, you do not remember what faith is anymore. It's all right because you were able to get yourself out of poverty. In addition, to raising your babies well, you have married a man that loves you. So, what is the point of church anyway? Why pray, when it feels like your life seems to be working out better than it did when you had put God first.

In a sense you still did put God first, just on your terms now.

People should be able to have a relationship with God, the way they want to, and not the way the church describes it to be. It does not have to be the way the Bible describes it as. That's your perspective now when it comes to your religion. It is more rejuvenating when your faith is built off of you.

Twenty years later, your son has dropped out of college. Your son has also had two babies, back to back, just like you did. Your son also has been in and out of prison.

Your daughter has graduated college, but she has caught AIDS. The doctors expect her to only have about two years left to live.

Your husband has cheated, once again. This time, however, your husband got his mistress pregnant.

So now, you went back to your home church and vowed to God to quit drinking, quit smoking, quit gambling, and change your life around.

Twenty-three years later, you are back to trusting God again, although your daughter has died.

Your husband left you for his mistress and their new baby.

Moreover, your son has to serve life in prison from a drug kingpin.

Your business went bankrupt, due to debt to the IRS. This also caused you to be evicted, since you left your two jobs since your business was flourishing, before.

You now live with a close friend.

Depression snuck into your life, like a silent killer. The trust you had in God, is quickly fading away. Nothing seems to take the pain and misery away.

It is twenty-six years later and you're now an alcohol addict. Drinking alcohol seems to numb the pain. Your parents always told you to trust God about your problems because he will fix it, but does he really? It seems as if God adds more to the problems. The scripture says, God will never put more on us than we can bear, but this pain feels unbearable. Life is weighing you down. You were doing so good, when you had the relationship with God your own way. The moment you came back to church, your life spiraled. It is as if every time you tell God yes to his will, life throws more rocks to knock you down.

It's now thirty years later, and you're now, not only an alcohol addict, but you're also a drug addict. Sniffing takes off the edge. Your body is craving anything to escape your misery. So, you give your body what it desires and it feels great.

Your friends and family called you to come over for dinner, when it was really an intervention. You were upset with your family, but you understood why they felt they needed to do an intervention.

While you stood in your parents living room, crying, you told everyone that you did not want the alcohol and drugs to control you anymore. The night before, your daughter visited you, in your dreams. She told you to let all of the toxins in your life go, before it destroys you, eventually killing you and your promise.

Your daughter is your guardian angel and you knew she was only sending a message from God.

So, as you continued standing in front of your family, while they did the intervention, you agreed to enter rehab. Your only preference is that the rehab center is a Christian rehab.

Your father, who is a minister, told you that that was already their intention. Your family wanted God to be in the center of your healing. They wanted a miracle to hit your life.

When you returned home, you fell to the floor and cried. Most nights you could not sleep, after losing your daughter and witnessing your son get put away in a cell for his life. Stress always ate away at your flesh.

You did not even mention to your family, at the intervention, the recent doctor's report you had received. The doctor had told you that you only had about two years to live, based on them identifying a tumor on your brain.

You stayed up all night because you did not want your daughter to tell you any more messages from God. You thought the next message would be about the brain tumor, so you packed your bags and watched tv.

The next morning, your father picked you up to take you to the rehab center. You were excited to change your life around.

When you were admitted into the rehab center, fear crept inside of you, consuming your mind. You tried to mingle and meet new friends, but the thoughts of fear had cluttered your vision.

So, when you went into your room, you told yourself, this will be another sleepless night.

The next morning, you went to play chess in the game room. You ended up making a new friend.

You and your new friend talked and laughed for hours.

As the days and months went by, you two became the best of friends.

One day, about a year later from entering rehab and twenty-eight years after the promise God gave you, your friend comes to knock on your door. She hands you a bible to keep. You told her many stories about how you love God, but some parts of your faith have faded away. So, this friend told you, open this bible up, once you become born again.

Your friend also loves God and believes it was his word that saved her life. So, you knew she was trying to help save yours, but you had no intentions of reading it anytime soon.

A few months later, the doctors called you to inform you that the report they had on your tumor was incorrect. You probably should have received more opinions from other doctors, anyway.

Twenty-nine years later, you left the rehab center.

As you left the rehab center, your family greeted you outside. Your dad smiled at you. You ran over to them and gave all of your family members hugs. You walked over to your dad and told your dad about the bible your friend had given you. You told him about how you were ready to visit church and let God back into your heart again. You were doing this not just for you, but for your children. Your dad's smile grew larger and he hugged you tightly. He kissed you on your forehead and said we can go this coming Sunday.

The following week, on Sunday, you went to church. Service was great and you went to the altar to get born again. You hoped to hear a prophetic message or catch the holy spirit, but that did not happen. Nevertheless, you were happy you still came to church.

After church, when you arrived back home, you called your friend you met in rehab. You told your friend from rehab how you went to church and gave your life back to Christ. Your friend was so excited to hear the news and started rejoicing over the phone.

After about three minutes of her rejoicing and you giggling, she began to grow silent. She proceeded to say, "You did not open the bible I gave you yet, did you?" You answered with a low, confused tone, "No I did not, but let me go get it now." You had placed your friend on hold while you went to open the bible, your friend had given to you while you were in rehab. You had opened the Bible and a ten-million-dollar check fell out, along with a deed to a house she had owned. The house was a five-bedroom house with six bedrooms, a two-car garage, a large front lawn, a deck and a backyard pool. Immediately you fell to the floor and began to cry. Your friend left a small note with these items stating, "The Lord told me to give this to you, once you had mentally recovered. All God wants is for you to say yes to trusting his will, with your whole heart."

While you were crying, you started rejoicing and speaking in your heavenly language, thanking God for his faithfulness.

You disconnected the phone to look your friend up on google, since you had no idea she was so wealthy. It turns out that your friend from rehab was a millionaire. Almost five years ago, she admitted herself into rehab due to being an alcoholic, as well.

In this moment, everything started to hit you all at once. The very second you told God yes, by giving your life back to Christ, God gave you his promise.

See, the first time you talked to God, when your children were small, God told you that you will receive a new home. Then you endured financial struggles that were designed to prepare you for the larger bills you would have. When you owned your business and worked two jobs, God prepared you to learn about valuing your time and money management. When you had a three-bedroom home, with two bathrooms, God prepared you to understand how to care for a home, so he could bless you with more. The moment you were married, God taught you how to treat those who do you wrong, gracefully. You told God yes again, thinking it was for your daughter to get well and your son to stop getting into trouble, when in reality, it was in that moment, that God wanted you to remember his promise.

God allowed the enemy to think he controlled you with alcohol and other toxins, when God knew it would lead you to his messenger, your friend from rehab.

Sadly, you realized you could have avoided the road your life led you into, if you trusted God's plan instead of altering his plan to get closer to your promise.

It does not matter how small you alter God's plan, even if it is simply getting two jobs to make ends meet. If you are not consistently asking God what is his plan for your life and how to align your plan with his plan, you will always wait longer for your promises.

In this story life was great at one point for this woman. Until many trials came to tear her down. The reality is our lives will always have trials and tribulations, but our trials and tribulations only come to make us stronger.

It is God's peace, mercy, love, favor, joy, hope, grace, and kindness that will sustain us.

Stay grounded in God and know when the worst battles in life come, they will not destroy you, like it did this woman.

Unfortunately, this woman in this story, waited twenty-nine years for her promise, when God did not intend for her to wait that long. All the woman had to do was be patient and listen to God's voice after she prayed. Her prayers and hearing from God, would have given her instructions on what to do, while she waited.

This parable was used to give wisdom and demonstrate how imperative it is to wait on God. I too, was like the woman in the story, but thanks be to God, I did not have to wait as long.

So, after Gerald confirmed the status of our relationship, I had so much joy!

Gerald would take me to beautiful restaurants, to the cinema, and shopping at the mall.

As much as Gerald and I enjoyed each other's company, I could still tell that his vibe was off. When Gerald and I were away from each other, he would barely call or text me. I had to initiate everything between us, including our date nights or inviting him to come over.

Gerald was very distant. When Gerald did come over, he barely even touched me. It was quite awkward. I would talk to my mom about how uncomfortable Gerald seemed to feel around me and she agreed his behavior was quite strange. So, I had convinced myself to hack into his Instagram page.

As I accessed his account on Instagram, Gerald was indeed, chatting and flirting with other women.

I contemplated if I should tell Gerald that I found out why his behavior had been thrown off, since my birthday was next week. Gerald and I did have plans for celebrating my birthday. I did not want to feel emotional, while being excited to celebrate my birthday, but I knew I could not settle for less.

So, I went ahead and told Gerald what I found on his Instagram account.

Of course, Gerald was in total denial. Instead, Gerald flipped the narrative on me, yelling at me because I invaded his privacy. Since he was upset that I secretly invaded his privacy, he broke up with me. Typical narcissistic behavior, right? Some of these men love to play reverse sociology, when in actuality they should be apologetic for their wrongs. Regardless of me hacking into his Instagram account, the truth will always reveal itself.

Gerald told me I could have just asked him for his password, but come on. Gerald was most certainly not going to give me his password.

The following week, on my birthday, Gerald posted the same woman that I found in messages, with a heart emoji on his Instagram story. To say I was hurt would be an understatement. I had never cried so hard in my entire life. I guess it hurt worse than my other breakups because Gerald was my best friend for years, before a relationship between us was even thought of. I just could not understand.

The day after my birthday, I reached out to Gerald and explained how I felt to him. Gerald stated that he had understood and we went out for lunch to further discuss how to move forward as friends. Our friendship bond was stuck together like gorilla glue, so we most definitely stayed friends.

The rest of the month of April, Gerald and I continued communicating and visiting each other almost every weekend. I started dating new men also.

Although I did notice a few other things between Gerald and I.

Whenever a new guy I would date called my telephone while Gerald was near, I would hurry and decline the call so Gerald did not see it. I would even hide my phone when Gerald would come over to my house to hang out. I even went to extreme measures, by blocking all the men in my phone who I dated, when I knew Gerald was coming over, so Gerald would not see them call or text. This identified to me that I still had strong feelings for Gerald, outside of our friendship. I just did not know if the feelings were mutual.

Until, one particular day, Gerald and I were hanging out at my house, watching movies and a guy I was dating had called my telephone. Gerald saw his name and picture appear on my phone screen and asked me, "Why does this guy always call you and who is he?" I responded, "I'm not sure why he keeps calling, but we are just friends, nothing else more."

Why was I lying to Gerald like this? Gerald stared at me, like a mean grizzly bear and said, Ok. Where did you meet this guy from? I bet you two are going on a date tomorrow." I giggled and said, "No not at all. In fact, why do you care? Gerald smiled and said, "Actuality, I do not."

Gerald left the conversation at that.

I knew Gerald cared, but he did not show it to me. It was only a matter of time before he could not hide his feelings anymore.

So, I kept the faith in knowing Gerald and I would be together very soon. It was at this moment that I learned how to have patience, even when I do not get the outcome I want.

God will give you, whatever your heart desires, through your patience. For the scripture says, in Isaiah 40 verse 31, "But those who trust in the Lord will find new strength. They will soar high on wings like eagles. They will run and not grow weary. They will walk and not faint."

The strength of God will help build your faith.

By the end of April 2020, Gerald and I were more than friends, at least it felt like it. We were intimate frequently. Gerald checked on me via text, every morning, afternoon and night. We held hands during car rides. Gerald would hold me by the waist, in public and even kiss me in front of others.

Sadly, during this month of May, my mom suffered from cancer and Covid-19, where she then became hospitalized. The doctors had almost pronounced her dead and she could not have visitors, due to the Covid-19 pandemic. My mom was 20% on the ventilator and her breathing rate was still dropping. Thank God that I had friends and family praying for her to live!

During this difficult time, Gerald stayed with me every single day, until my mom came home from the hospital. My mom stayed in the hospital for almost two months. Gerald would allow me to use his vehicle whenever I needed to, he would buy groceries for me, he gave me money, he held me tightly while I cried each and every night, and so much more. He truly supported me in a way no one has done for me before.

By the time my mom's health had started to swiftly improve, Gerald started to grow a little distant again. Not as bad as before, but he was still unusual. I was not sure why. I honestly had thought by the way Gerald supported me, that we were in a relationship.

So, one night when Gerald came over to my place, I asked him for clarity. While Gerald and I cuddled in bed, I asked him, "What is our relationship status?" Gerald remained quiet for about two minutes, which made me nervous and said, "Ebony, I care about you a lot and my feelings for you are real, but I cannot lie to you, I like talking to other women also. Different women bring different vibes. However, out of all the women I see and talk to, you are my favorite. I am just not ready to be fully committed right now. I hope you can understand, without feeling the need to end what we have."

Now usually, I would catch an attitude, tell him to leave and block him, but for some reason I respected his honesty this time.

By early June, my mom came home! Gerald met with me and my stepmom at the hospital my mom stayed at, while we waited for my mom to leave the hospital. We all rejoiced when my mom came out of the hospital and Gerald bought my mom some food she was craving for weeks inside of the hospital. See, Gerald always knows what to do, to keep my heart locked to his.

As the weeks went by, my mom would always ask, "What's going on between you and Gerald?" I would always tell her that Gerald and I were only friends. My mom respected that answer, shockingly.

Gerald was still spending the night, when my mom was back home from the hospital. Gerald was sleeping in my room and no longer on the couch. Now if you have strict parents, you would know, most parents would only want your boyfriend spending the night, not your friend. Some strict parents do not let boyfriends spend the night at all! The type of mom I have, she did not let any man spend the night, besides my child's father and that was only because he had to help with our baby.

Gerald and I had no child together and were not in a relationship, but yet my mom wanted Gerald to always come over to spend the night. My mom would invite Gerald over, herself. It was not me who told Gerald to stop sleeping on the couch, it was her. My mom not only told Gerald he could sleep in my room, but we kept the door cracked open to still give her respect and she would ask us, why did we have the door opened. She told us to shut it. Did the doctor swipe my mom's brain or something? Instantly, I knew Gerald was special.

Although Gerald and I were not in a relationship, I knew I could depend on him for anything. Besides, Gerald always answered my call on the first ring.

By the end of June, I think I had fallen in love with Gerald.

I had invited Gerald to come to my cousin's wedding with me. My family loved Gerald. Of course, they asked if he was my boyfriend. I told my family Gerald was not my boyfriend and shockingly, they respected that also.

My family treated Gerald like he was their blood.

Gerald, my family, my mom and her wife danced and had a joyous time that day of my cousin's wedding.

Later that evening, Gerald invited me to come with him to his sister's birthday party. I thought my family loved Gerald. Gerald's family had treated me ten times better! Gerald's sisters and brothers became my siblings the moment we met. Of course, I knew them when we were friends, but when we went to his sister's birthday party, it had a different vibe. Different, in a great way. His siblings and I danced and laughed the night away. It was from that day, seeing how much our families loved us together, I knew the time was surely coming for when we will finally make our relationship official.

The next day, Gerald and I went to the beach to relax. We laid on the sand talking about life.

While Gerald and I soaked up the sun, on the beach, a man walked up to me saying he remembered me from school. I could tell the man had a crush on me the way he looked at me. The anger in Gerald had in his eyes, made me laugh out loud. The man then walked away. I began apologizing to Gerald, still giggling. I asked Gerald why did he roll his eyes when the man approached me. He responded that he does not know why that guy had to mention that or even approach us in the first place. I personally thought it was very cute.

I knew at this moment Gerald had fallen in love with me also.

Along came the fourth of July weekend.

Gerald had invited me to come to his cousin's mansion for that weekend.

Gerald's cousin had a big pool in his backyard and a jacuzzi indoors. His cousin's house was like the house of Belair.

When Gerald and I had arrived at his cousin's mansion, Gerald introduced me as his friend to his family. Shockingly, they loved the fact that we were honest about our friendship status. In fact, because Gerald and I were so honest, Gerald's family wanted me to keep coming back over.

While Gerald and I laid down in our guest room, at his cousin's mansion, I asked Gerald our status, once again. Gerald's response was, "I do not understand why you keep asking Eb, the status is not changing, we are just friends." I responded, "One thing we are not going to do Gerald, is play childish games! We've spent so much time together, making beautiful memories and pretending as if we are blinded to the love we share. If you do not want a relationship, once we leave here tomorrow, do not talk to me anymore. Gerald stared at me, looked down with pity and said "Ok, that is fine."

If you are a man reading this book, please do yourself and myself a favor. Please stop being stubborn! Women as well! A lot of us individuals know what we want, but are often too stubborn to go after it. Stubbornness is attached to fear, pride, past trauma, low self-esteem, rejection, emotional damage, and more.

However, please realize when you allow stubbornness to get in your way, it will block your blessings, ultimately blocking your promise. Some of you may say, "Well, I'm often stubborn, but I'm still blessed." Which could be very true, but you could be further. You could have had your dream husband or wife, your dream house, your dream job, your dream car, had that stubborn trait and everything attached to it, was removed.

My point is, Gerald went through a lot of hurt and emotional damage, from me cutting him off, all because he was stubborn. The truth is, the hurt Gerald had experienced was honestly Gerald hurting himself because of his own fears. Remember, our bible tells us in 2 Timothy 1 verse 7, For God has not given us the spirit of fear and timidity, but of power, love and self-discipline.

The important factor here is that these negative traits allow the devil to have access to us. Ultimately controlling us, in a sense. We give the enemy power when we choose to have fear and the rest of the negative traits attached to stubbornness. This power we give to the devil will make us weak, it will make us lose some of our blessings, allowing us to feel defeated and could even cause us to kill ourselves. All because of the hurt we feel. Allowing the enemy to know he's doing great at his job, which is stealing, killing and destroying.

Say this prayer with me,

> *Lord, release your power over me! I rebuke the enemy over my life. The devil gets no power from me! We give you all the power, God, because it belongs to you! You said in your word father, that because you are the*

greatest power, that I shall never be defeated. I am more than a conqueror, through Christ, that strengthens me! The battle is not mine, it is yours God. Help me to fight in every trial and tribulation I endure and help me to win each battle! I will win! I will never lose, for your blood shed over me, never loses its power. Thank you for your blood God! Thank you for your power God! **In Jesus name, Amen.**

After that day, when I had returned back home, Gerald and I no longer spoke. I knew I had to sit back and watch everything unravel.

Six days later, after still not speaking to Gerald, Gerald showed up at my house. So, backtrack a little, I called Gerald earlier this day, because I had a terrible argument with my child's father and my child's father's family. It resulted in my child's father's family trying to physically assault me. When I called Gerald, explaining to him everything that was going on, he asked if I was ok and told me he would protect me if anyone did anything to me. Gerald then proceeded to tell me how he was already around the corner from my house at the casino and planned on coming to see me anyway. Gerald asked me if I wanted anything from the store before he came over and we hung up the telephone.

As soon as we disconnected our phone, Gerald was at my doorstep.

I opened the door for him and greeted him with a hug.

Gerald and I walked over to the living room and sat on the couch. I had my five-year-old laying down on the couch also because I was trying to put him asleep. I picked my son up, and rocked him asleep, while chatting with Gerald. I was telling Gerald how chaotic the day was and how nothing was accomplished for my son's graduation tomorrow, due to that argument I was in earlier.

The entire time I was talking, Gerald leaned towards me, gazing into my eyes. I started to get butterflies in my belly. I started stuttering and making gulps while I was talking. I am sure Gerald identified how nervous I was, but he kept smiling so I assumed he had thought me becoming nervous, was cute.

Once my son had fallen asleep, I stood up and told Gerald I would be right back.

I went into my bedroom and tucked my son on my bed. I came back into the living room to sit on the couch with Gerald.

I went back to talking about the commotion that went on earlier that day and how excited I was for my son to graduate pre-k.

While I was talking his head off, Gerald slowly grabbed me, while still gazing into my eyes and kissed me. Gerald and I kissed passionately for about six minutes.

When we stopped kissing, he had asked me to lay down with him on the couch.

I laid down with Gerald and he said look at me, "I want to talk to you about a few things."

Immediately, I grew nervous even more. I responded, "Ok, what's up?", in a soft, timid tone. Gerald said to me, I want us to be together, but for some reason I'm afraid. I have never felt this way about someone before. The way I care about you, runs deep. I have been asking all of my friends every day, what's wrong with me? Ebony is everything a man would want in a woman, but I keep holding myself back from being with her."

While Gerald continued to confess his feelings towards me, my heart smiled.

This was a pure example of how God will fight your battles for you. All I had to do was sit back, pray my way through, and be patient while I waited.

When females know a man cares for them, but plays childish games, females take matters into their own hands. Females will tell these men off and tell them they are a fool to play games with them. Females get aggressive or upset because their emotions overwhelm them and ultimately get the best of them. Females even try to get back even with men by dating other men to prove their feelings are not attached.

Women, please stop doing all of these things. It makes us women look just as foolish as these men! Why? Simple because the bible states, vengeance is the Lord's! Anyone that has ever done you wrong, will always get what they deserve in return. Even if that person that has done you wrong never gets their karma back to them, understand that God is working on them behind the scenes. If you are a woman, seeking answers like I did, just sit back and wait on God. The same rule applies for you men also!

God will always reveal to you, what you need to know, when you need to know it. God will either tell you to move forward with a task or sit back and wait. Trust God's process. I know it is easier said than done, but remember our life challenges are never meant to be easy or else the world would have no evil in it.

Everyone would be successful and happy, if life was meant to be easy. If life were meant to be easy, none of us would even be here on earth. Everything in our life serves a purpose, the good and the bad. That is why it is crucial to see God in everything we do. Yes, every single thing you see and do. See God when you simply cook dinner at home or when you tie your shoe, because when you see God in everything, you'll understand God is always speaking to you. He's waiting for you to listen so that he can direct your path. God wants to give you instructions, while you wait for whatever it is that you are seeking from him.

We have to start acknowledging God more. We cannot just acknowledge God when we feel like it, but wonder why we are stuck in certain seasons of our lives. We cannot just acknowledge him when we pray or when we go to church. We cannot just acknowledge him when we noticed one day last week he showed us a sign. No! God is ALWAYS showing you a sign! Not just that one day, you caught yourself paying attention. God is speaking, each and every second, every moment. Simply, just acknowledge him.

After listening to everything Gerald had said, I said, "Well, let's be together then. Gerald responded, "I truly want to say yes, but then again it feels like I cannot tell you yes." I grew tired of this phase we kept going through, and said, "We can just drop this discussion." So, that is exactly what we did.

The next morning Gerald took me to the mall to buy my son an outfit and a pair of shoes for his graduation. My son's father could no longer buy my son's outfit for the graduation or attend due to us arguing, so Gerald said he would step up on my son's father's behalf.

It is moments like this that made me love Gerald even more.

Gerald and I arrived at my son's graduation and we cheered him on while my son received all his awards. It was like Gerald and I were proud parents. Gerald had his camera held in his hand, capturing photos of my son and videos of him. Gerald was a proud stepfather.

It's one thing when a man loves you, but it's a greater feeling when a man cares for your child.

When Gerald, my son and I left my son's graduation, Gerald and I put together a party for my son in my backyard. Gerald gave me his car keys and told me to use his card to get whatever decorations, cake, or food I had needed, before everyone arrived. This was something my child's father's family was supposed to do, but did not, due to the argument we had the day before. While I ran out to get everything needed for my son's graduation party, Gerald stayed at my house cleaning and prepping before everyone arrived.

Just by how Gerald had my back, I knew in my heart, he would be my husband one day.

My son's graduation party was phenomenal. My son had a blast. Gerald and I made sure my son had the best graduation celebration ever. All of our friends and family came to celebrate and it was a joyous occasion.

Late that evening, Gerald invited me to go to a party with him and his sisters. I asked my mom to look after my son since his little cousins were spending the night with him after his graduation party.

I was on cloud nine from how Gerald stepped up to the plate to ensure that I was happy.

While Gerald and I drove to the party, I grabbed his hand. He looked at me and smiled. I asked him, "So, now does this mean we are officially a couple?" He laughed and said, "What made you ask me that?" I responded with a frustrated tone, throwing his hand away from mines, "Do you not remember our conversation we had last night?" Gerald said, "Ok, number one, calm yourself down. Number two, I told you specifically that I was not sure. I am still not sure. Let's just remain friends. Ok?"

Then I began to cry. He said, "Eb, come on, do not start crying. I am sorry." I told Gerald, "No, all of this is just hurtful. It's a tug of war game being played with my heart and it is not fair Gerald! Just forget it! Let's have fun at this party."

I had to control my feelings because we were arriving at the party and his sisters were standing outside waving at us. I knew the problem was never me, it was Gerald. So, I threw my feelings in the trash and told myself I am going to enjoy myself. I probably should have taken notes from myself tonight because it would have saved me from a lot of fights Gerald and I would face in our future.

Gerald and I had an amazing time at the party. We ate delicious food, had some spiked beverages, danced on the dance floor, took pictures and laughed the night away. When Gerald and I were leaving out, his uncle walked up to him and asked him who I was. Gerald took a deep breath, smiled and said, "This is my girlfriend, Ebony." His uncle shook my hand and said, "It is a pleasure to meet my nephew's girlfriend. You two make a beautiful couple."

When Gerald's uncle had walked away, I whispered in Gerald's ear, "So you meant that?" Gerald laughed, saying, "Yeah. I cannot fight it any longer. I know for a fact I want to be with you." Then Gerald and I kissed, held hands and went home to my house.

Every day, after that night Gerald and I were inseparable. We were traveling out of the state going on baecation trips. We had each other's pictures on our social media platforms. We became foodies going to new restaurants every other day. We were so adventurous, going to places like indoor skydiving, axe throwing, painting with a twist, amusement parks, we even went on a cruise.

What's sad is that the happy phase in the beginning of a relationship does not last longer than the hard-argumentative phase. At least, it does not feel like it. Or should I honestly say, the devil does not want us to enjoy the happy phase.

Never get too consumed in your own happiness, that you forget to stay prayed up. Most importantly, do not get too consumed into your own happiness, that you forget, just as much as God is on assignment, so he is the enemy. Not only is the devil on assignment, he brings serpents to appear within your circle.

I definitely became a victim of this.

Why is it that we all want a seat at the table, but cannot handle that our enemies will be seated at the table also? God's word tells us in Psalms 23 verse 5, You prepare a feast for me in the presence of my enemies. You honor me by anointing my head with oil. My cup overflows blessings.

As individuals, we all want our circle to include people that are close to us. If you are in a season where you are surrounded by enemies, or have just one enemy that seems to always appear, understand that God is preparing you to sit at your table. Your table will always represent that it is your harvest season!

We have to stop saying we only want people who are good to us, people we can trust, people who are our friends, people we love, etc., to only be a part of our circle and our harvest. No! If you are headed for greatness, your circle and your harvest will ALWAYS have some enemies within. Let God prepare your table. Stop taking it amongst ourselves to remove people we do not want at the table. In addition to the table representing your success, it will also represent your success. We cannot be successful, pushing our enemies away. Moreover, do not let this make you think that you should leave the table because your table will always have your promise attached to it. We have come too far in life, to ever abandon our promise!

A couple months after Gerald and I made our relationship official, Gerald's ex came back around in his life. This was the same ex that had cheated on Gerald, aborted his baby she was pregnant with, left Gerald for the man she cheated on him with and had a baby with the man she cheated on Gerald with. Instead of aborting that baby, she kept it with the man she cheated with. It is sad right? The unbelievable part is when Gerald went through this heartbreak, I was there for him each day.

When Gerald found out she had cheated on him, he called me and cried.

You are probably thinking, well, this answers why Gerald was afraid to be with you. Actually, no, it does not.

Although Gerald's ex caused a lot of emotional damage to him, they still remained good friends.

I never liked the concept of exes remaining friends. It never sits right with me.

Gerald's ex taught him forex.

Forex is trading currencies within the foreign exchange market. It is an easy way to make fast money. If you are a great trader, you can easily make over six figures, but it takes a lot of practice and studying charts.

Gerald loved forex more than anything in this world. He loved it because of how great he was at this skill. Gerald was consistently making money every single week, more so on a daily basis. I saw Gerald flip ten dollars into one hundred dollars, on numerous occasions. I even witnessed Gerald flipping one hundred dollars into four-teen hundred dollars.

Now Gerald's ex, was a mastermind at forex. She was friends with some of the biggest traders in the country. So, Gerald leaned on her for informative tools to always become a better trader.

I tried to ignore my feelings when it came to Gerald working with his ex.

When Gerald and I would ride in his car, his ex often called. Gerald would inform her that he was out with me, but she would careless. Gerald's ex would text him after they hung up on the phone, "Hurry up and go home, so we can study up on forex."

Whenever Gerald would spend the night at my house, his ex would call or text him late at night trying to discuss forex. She even sent him a picture of her getting her hair done. Now do not think I did not address what she was doing, because I definitely did. In fact, Gerald and I argued over his ex on numerous occasions, and we even had short breakups.

Often, I would cry to my friends, Gerald's friends, my family, and Gerald's family, just venting about the chaos his ex was causing. No one seemed to view it as horrible as I did, but when I would ask if they would stay with someone who was close friends with their ex, they would say, absolutely not!

I guess the reason I stayed with Gerald is because he gave me security.

I knew his passwords to his social media outlets, his phone, his email, his computer and had his location on my phone, as a tracker. He gave me these passwords, of course.

Gerald had nothing to hide from me, but what I truly wanted was sacrifice.

One of the reasons a relationship can last long is because of the sacrifices that were made to keep it.

Gerald chose not to make sacrifices, but we did stay together. At least for a nice period of time.

Gerald created boundaries with his ex. He sent her messages in front of me to inform his ex that certain things will no longer be allowed out of respect to his relationship. For example, Gerald told her that she could not call or text him past nine o'clock at night. Did she respect that? Absolutely, not!

So, I told Gerald I would handle his ex myself.

When I addressed Gerald's ex, she caught an attitude with me, telling me that I should be more confident in myself.

When Gerald found out that I had sent his ex-text messages telling her how disrespectful she was, Gerald became upset with me.

Gerald and I argued for a week straight.

By the end of that week, Gerald's little sister had a pop-up shop event. Gerald and I were originally supposed to meet earlier in the day, but another argument broke out between us and Gerald ignored me the entire day.

Once I arrived at Gerald's little sister event, Gerald tried to act as if I did not exist. So, I gladly walked over to Gerald, yelling and telling him off, even in front of my son. My emotions took full reign over me.

Someone at the event had to tell Gerald and I to go outside, while they looked after my son, due to how we started arguing.

This was a sign of danger for us.

After talking to Gerald, for approximately forty-five minutes, Gerald and I had finally come to an agreement. I gave Gerald an ultimatum. It was either me or his ex. If Gerald needed to think about this long and hard, he made his decision.

Gerald told me he chose me, but he really did not.

The next day Gerald was supposed to come over and he did not. I called Gerald about five times. No answer. I sent Gerald about ten long paragraph messages, still no response. Gerald actually, left my text messages on read, which is one of the worst feelings; when someone is intentionally ignoring you and that someone happens to be someone you love.

I sent Gerald voice audios, still no response.

I started having a mental breakdown from everything I endured with Gerald. I feel as if I am always getting hurt. This could not be love. If it is, I did not want it.

After hours of crying in my car, he sent a text message saying that he was moving forward and for some reason that was more refreshing than being ignored. I had peace knowing where we stood. It was hurtful still, but it was well needed.

To every reader, reading this book, find the beauty in what has hurt you. Not everything bad that happens comes from the devil. Sometimes the worst things that break us mentally, was something that God did. We give too much power to the devil, as I stated before, then we give to God.

God is always trying to grab our attention. The moment you pray and ask God to rebuke the enemy over your life, you are already protected from Satan's attacks. For the bible says, in Psalms 34 verse 7, For the angel of the Lord is a guard: he surrounds and defends all who fear him.

Angels are protecting you! Stop thinking that car accident, that job you lost, that bad doctor's report was from the enemy, when it was from God. It was designed for you to hear what God is saying, because as the song says, in the movie, The Color Purple, God is always trying to tell you something. God is always talking, we have to decide when we want to listen.

It was in this moment of Gerald breaking my heart, that God began to give me specific instructions.

God told me, "Gerald was in love with me and it made Gerald afraid. Gerald is afraid of love because of how love has hurt him since his childhood. The hurt runs deep. There's a tree of hurt and rejection in him. Gerald was also insecure of himself. Gerald tried to love others, when they stabbed him each time. Gerald had to make himself try to love again, but fear overwhelms him. It was never you. It was always Gerald running from his problems. Something we all do or have already done."

Now Gerald never told me any of what God told me, or told me that he loves me yet. I always wanted to hear Gerald say it, because I felt the love in our relationship, but since Gerald broke up with me, I felt defeated.

However, God revealed to me that it was only a matter of time before Gerald told the truth of what he was running from and that he was in love with me. God told me Gerald would come to my door and say it to my face. I knew I had to just be patient and know that God will never bring me far, just to leave me. For God said in his word, in Deuteronomy 31 verse 8, Do not be afraid or discouraged, for the Lord will personally go ahead of you. He will be with you; he will neither fail nor abandon you. So, my faith was up!

I waited. I prayed. I fasted. I did not fast because I wanted my results quickly, I fasted because the strength I needed could only come from God. I needed a strength I never had, a peace I never experienced and wisdom that would help me understand clearer.

When and if you are going through a difficult season in your life and you need more income, more friends, love, a car, a house, do not just fast for an expectation. Fast to get the internal blessings that ONLY God can give. It will actually help you to overcome sooner, because it equips you to remain focused on God's agenda. Your stress will no longer attack your health because of God's peace. The doctor will notice the improvement in your body, based on God's joy! For the word of God says in Nehemiah 8 verse 10, Don't be dejected and sad, for the joy of the Lord is your strength!

The joy does not come from toxins. Joy, at least the right joy, comes from God. If you can grasp this quickly, expect God to move quickly on your behalf.

While you wait for God to move on your behalf, thank God and praise God for who he is, what he has done, and what is about to do for you. The scripture says, in Psalms 100 verse 4, Enter into his gates with thanksgiving; go into his courts with praise. Give thanks to him and praise his name.

Listen, David, did not give this acrimony just to simply rejoice. David was teaching us how to get what we need from God. If you need God to move, read the book of Psalms. If you do what David said in the word of God, you allow God to open up the gates of heaven to release his blessings upon you on earth.

Whatever the circumstance may be, do not complain. God hates when we complain and he will make you wait longer for whatever it is you are asking him for. You might just miss your blessing or your promise, if you continue to complain.

After hearing what God told me about Gerald, I worshiped. I trusted God. I cried, but I pushed through.

At the end of that week, Gerald blew my phone up, begging me if we could meet up and talk about why he had done what he did in his car.

I told Gerald he could meet me when I returned back home.

As soon as I arrived home, he was in his car waiting for me.

When I sat in Gerald's car, he told me "I am in love with you Ebony." He even began to get emotional, wiping away his tears, saying, "The problem was never you, it was me. I am insecure about myself and I did not want to put my insecurities or my fears on you. I have been through so much hurt and I did not want my hurt affecting you. I know I am still wrong for everything I put you through, but you taught me how to not fear love. I can be myself around you. You are beautiful inside and out.

Even if you decide you do not want to be with me, I will go get the help and counsel I need to become a better man for you. For us. I love you."

As Gerald sat in the driver's seat, confessing his love for me, all I could think about was how close my relationship with God has grown to be. It is closer than I could ever imagine. I knew God was real and he speaks, but come on. God speaks this clearly? I had to take in this moment.

Later that week, Gerald and I were back in a relationship. Now who would have thought, in that year of October 2020 we would have such a traumatic breakup. Just to have an even worse break up this year of October 2022.

The breakup of October 2022, is what Chapter one, of this book, is about.

Great things come in threes. God will always prepare you for what season you are walking into. This whole month of October, 2022, the song, "Something Great, Something Big", by Kurt Carr continues to play around me. My church choir had sung this song, for our church anniversary, which was October 31, 2022.

Although Gerald and I have been through so many trials and tribulations, I do not feel defeated. 2023 is the year of greatness!

God showed me, me leaving my job, a new house, Gerald and I engaged, me flourishing with my business, and more. God even showed me becoming a millionaire in 2023.

I just have to trust God's process.

Sincerely,
Trusting with a Purpose

Chapter 11

A PURPOSEFUL CHANGE

DAY 11

Dear Diary,   *December 27, 2022*

You may be wondering why I never discussed what clicked to me in the previous chapter and drifted into my past story with Gerald. I did not discuss what clicked to me because I wanted readers to understand how my thought process flows. I had to remember what I had already gone through with Gerald in my past, to help to understand why Gerald and I were back in the same place, in our present.

Here's a gem for all readers, your past will always have meaning for your future. Do not turn back to the old you, but use the old you to help with the new decision you make. Your past will always have value. Some of your past has more value than your future. You can let go of the past damage, hurt, trauma, bitterness, stress, depression, etc., but do not abandon your past, because this is where purpose comes in.

Understanding your purpose or what serves a meaningful purpose in your life can be tricky. I had taken my time with learning this concept.

What had clicked to me back in the previous beginning chapter was Gerald's purpose on why he is the way he is, which was his past. As I mentioned in the previous chapter of how Gerald's past hurt and trauma ultimately affected his decision making. The thing is, Gerald allowed his past to serve a negative purpose in his life, versus serving a positive one.

Gerald's past hurt, rejection, abandonment, traumas, ultimately, made him afraid to love and caused him to have low self-esteem issues. When the purpose God wanted those past trials, Gerald suffered with was to be healed, to have confidence, help others to overcome, and most importantly, forgive.

It is important that we ask God to help us understand the purpose in why we went through situations in our life. Remember I stated in the previous chapter that not all attacks come from the devil. In fact, a lot of our attacks come from God. Some of us know that and some of us do not. Those that understand this concept, get upset with God, at times. Stop being upset with God for the mess in your life and understand the purpose in which the mess serves!

I knew if Gerald never understood the positive aspect in which his purpose served, I had to play the song, You Know My Name, by Tasha Cobbs, to remember that God has meaning behind my name. If you ever listen to this song, you'll understand why this song is necessary to play when you do not understand why you are going through a difficult time. God knows your name, he knows all about what you are going through and he will walk with you to bring you out of the darkness and into his light. He will turn your brokenness into beauty!

As I lifted my hands, while I sat on my bed, I began to sing the lyrics to this song out loud. While the tears began to fall down my face, God began to tell me that he has never forgotten about me. God told me that he would never leave me, nor forsake me. God said, "Ebony, you have won this battle! Ebony, you entered victory!" When God spoke that over me, I began to cry like an infant wanting a bottle of warm milk. I was rejoicing and praising God for his marvelous works! I'll tell you why.

After Gerald's and I breakup back in October of 2020, the previous chapter story, Gerald and I did get back together. Gerald and I were in a great place! Gerald and I were so in love that we were preparing to move in together.

During that time, my mom's landlord was making us leave in two months' notice due to renovations the house needed. I immediately called Gerald, panicking about what was going to happen and he found us a new place within that day. Also, during this time, I was dealing with a custody battle with my son's father. The judge had informed me that wherever I lived, that my son would need his own bedroom, a car, and the home to have my name on it. Not only did Gerald help me with fixing up my son's bedroom and getting our place together, but Gerald also helped me to get a new car. A brand-new car at that. Gerald paid someone to paint my son's room, Spiderman themed, he bought my son a bed that came with a dresser and night stand, and more.

I was always used to my mom always supporting me and not anyone else. So, it was odd, having another person do so much for me, but I was thankful.

Fast forwarding into the next year, 2021, in February, Gerald and I had moved into our new home.

The move in was completely stressful to say the least and for the first two months of living together, Gerald and I argued almost every day. It was an adjustment because I was only used to living with my mom, stepmom, and my son.

As much as I wanted to leave the nest one day, I never pictured myself moving out of my mom's house in reality. I guess because I was the only child, which made me the true definition of a *mama's girl*. So, there was a lot of fear inside of me once Gerald and I moved into our own home together.

I figured due to my fear of readjusting my life, this was why Gerald and I argued so much.

However, I was wrong.

As the months grew, Gerald argued more and more.

I believe the arguments stemmed from finances.

Gerald loved to take care of my son and I, but keeping a job was difficult for Gerald. Jobs had come and went, left and right. Depression entered Gerald from these jobs and it trickled over to me.

By the end of the year, 2021, Gerald had approximately seven jobs in one year.

My new year's resolution was that for 2022, Gerald and I's financial situation would get better. I prayed for no more struggling to make ends meet. No more living paycheck to paycheck. No more late bill notices.

Although I had a great job, working for the IRS, I still needed more support, financially. My income was not enough to pay rent, utility bills, a car note, car insurance, groceries, phone bills, and most importantly provide for my son. It was at this moment I lacked acknowledging my full potential.

On January 1, of 2022, Gerald and I went to church.

Our Pastor called us both to the altar for prayer and told us that there was a corporate blessing in store for us.

Gerald and I, received the word spoken over us, rejoiced and thanked God for his word that was spoken over us.

When Gerald and I returned back to our seats, our pastor said, "For someone in this room, God is getting ready to make them into a millionaire next year."

Everyone in the congregation rejoiced, but she said this word was only for one person in particular.

She then went on to say, she had almost wanted the person to come to the altar.

Everyone looked around.

I assumed she was talking about some of the business owners that are within the congregation. I had no idea, but I knew it was not me.

The next morning, my pastor called me saying, "The person I was referring to being a millionaire in the room was you." When she said this to me I was stunned. This was not the first time or second time a pastor has spoken this prophetic word over me, but to receive it, is always mind blowing.

After I hung the phone up, from talking about becoming a millionaire, I asked God, what did I need to do to become a millionaire this year. God did not say anything back to me, at least nothing that I wanted to hear. So, I started a skincare company.

I spent hours each and every day, teaching myself chemistry, while working my nine to five job.

I received my LLC, EIN, Trademark, vendor's license, DUNS Number, business email, etc.

In addition, I had a logo created, bought packaging and ingredients to formulate my products.

I sacrificed hanging out with friends on weekends to study and produce my business.

I needed more money to flow in so I could make my product top notch quality, so I went back to college, full time, in March, 2022 to finish my business degree. While also picking up a second job on campus and doing uber eats.

Gerald still struggled with jobs, sadly, that at this point he was not working at all. Gerald's car was repossessed, his phone was turned off, credit score dropped rapidly and had so many car tickets, that a warrant was almost issued for Gerald.

Due to Gerald owing so many car ticket bills, his license was taken from him.

While I worked like a hog and mule, I would always come home to Gerald either playing his video games each day and him drinking alcohol often.

Gerald's depression made him unproductive and our relationship was slowly turning downhill.

Gerald began turning into an alcoholic.

He had a lot of close relatives, including his father, that were alcoholics so I feared this for him. I am a quitter, so I aimed to stay determined for my relationship with Gerald, but this was not how I had pictured our life going.

One day, while Gerald was out, searching for new jobs, I sat in the bathroom, crying and talking to God. I asked God, "Why am I here? Why is my life like this? I serve in my church. I pay my tithes and offerings, each and every Sunday! I never miss a Sunday of church or bible study. I fast and I pray consistently. I intercede for others. Tell me God, why am I here? I just do not understand. You said in your word God, in Lamentations 3 verse 23, Great is his faithfulness: Here I am being faithful to you, even on days I am weak. I always put you first in my life. There are days I want to quit not just on you, but on myself but I always praise you, despite how I feel. Why do you have me here? I feel emotionally drained. I am physically drained. I am tired of being tired. Why am I here God?"

Have you ever been in a season where you were faithful to God, but he still has you in the pit? A pit of misery. A pit of depression. A pit of stress and frustration. A pit of sadness.

Sometimes these pits enter our lives, to birth out greatness. A pit is very similar to a stomach. Sometimes it may be filled and sometimes it is empty. Some of us need our pit cleaned. The moment God starts to clean out our pits, it is when our life will feel like a storm hit.

Trust God's process.

When God cleanses our pits, he births something out of us, in the process.

God told me, "The storm is not coming for you, it is coming for Gerald. Both you and Gerald will be happily married, very soon, once the storm passes over. The storm will feel long, but your happiness will be longer. Honestly, Gerald is ready to marry you now, but I need you to wait for my timing because this next season you are getting ready to enter will feel like an emotional roller coaster, that will send your mind through loops. This roller coaster will have the power to either make or break you. If you hold on to my hand, I will bless you whether Gerald leaves or stays. I am always watching how faithful you are to me. I love how you put me first Ebony. Keep running the course! The reward will blow your mind"

After I had this talk with God I felt rejuvenated. God gave me strength to hold on. What I did not know was that holding on would mean I had to learn how to walk with God alone. Meaning, I had to handle bills alone. I had to vent only to God. I had to eliminate everyone around me and trust God on a higher level. Sadly, I did not know this would also cause me to become Gerald's verbal punching bag. I suffered emotional abuse.

I began putting my dreams, my goals, and my wishes on hold for Gerald to get back up on his feet again. Not only was I handling all of Gerald's and I bills on my own, but I was also buying Gerald clothes, shoes, paying for haircuts, giving him my car, etc. I wanted to show him how much of a rider I truly was. I did it all, while working full time, being a mother, full time student, and entrepreneur. I was so stressed out that I, too, had become an alcoholic.

You know, sometimes, all it takes is for you to put your hand out for someone else, just for you to fall down on your face.

Instead of getting the favor you have done for them in return, they pull all your fingers off your hand.

Next, they are pulling your arms out of sockets.

Once, your arms are gone, now you're breaking your legs for them.

You are turning your head for them so much, that you're cracking your neck, to the point your head falls off.

Now, sadly, you have now fallen completely apart and when you need them to help fix your own broken body pieces that they ripped apart, they are nowhere to be found.

Well, actually, they are found, but they choose to watch you fix your own self, while they enjoy their lives.

You have to mend your own broken pieces, that they tore apart.

Unfortunately, we have all been here, on both ends.

My advice to those who have or are experiencing someone ripping them apart like this is to never let anyone tear you apart like this again!

The more you allow people to repeatedly damage your body parts, they will begin to take more than they did before. For example, taking your heart, your eyes (vision), your brain (your mind), and these things, unfortunately, are NOT easily fixable.

If you lose your heart and your brain there's a likely chance of death or never being the same again.

Now how God will use these situations, like when someone makes us break our legs. God will change the way we walk, to walk in his image.

When we have our fingers and hands broken, God will give us new hands to put forth to do.

God has no intention of taking your heart, to not allow you to love again. God has no intention of taking your vision, to make you blinded to your promise he gave you. God has no intention of taking your mind, to cause a lifetime of trauma.

Let God fix you. Do not try to fix yourself. Let God change you.

God knows all about the people that tore you apart and how they watched you try to mend together your pieces. He remembers how they intentionally tried to destroy you, externally and internally. God remembers how they almost tried to even kill you, physically and emotionally.

God has not forgotten!

Even if you are still stuck, waiting on God to fix you, God knows and he cares.

This is why, as I stated in the beginning of this chapter, I played the song, He knows my name, by Tasha Cobbs. Not only does this song minster in lyrics, by saying "Oh how you walk with me and oh how you talk to me", but the song goes on to say, "I am walking in your victory, because your power lives within me, no giant can stop me, because you hold my hand."

Never underestimate these powerful gospel songs! They are impacted with so much power! Play songs that have the power to speak to your situation. I promise, these gospel songs will give you peace in the middle of the storm you are in.

Later that evening, after I sang Tasha Cobb's song, Gerald called me apologizing for everything he ever put me through. Gerald sent me proof that he paid for us to begin counseling as soon as possible. Gerald begged me all night to go back to fixing us. He made reservations for us to talk over dinner and expressed his love for me. Gerald had asked me if we could spend the next couple of days together and I said yes.

God showed me that I had crossed over into victory after I sang Tasha Cobb's song. This battle I had fought these past couple of days, I fought spiritually, through prayer, every single day until I won. Not only did God change me, but he changed Gerald.

After Gerald and I hung up the phone, God put on my heart the song, "Change me" by Tamela Mann, again. I hope to encourage you readers, by saying, while you wait for unanswered prayers, blessings, promises, allow God to change you first. Sometimes we will wait longer for what we are asking God for because we are not allowing God to change us in order to get ready to receive what we are asking for. The moment you let God change you, you allow God to move quickly on your behalf. As Tamela Mann sang, her lyrics said, "Change me oh God, make me more like you."

Let God change you.

Sincerely,
A Changed Woman

Chapter 12

A NEW SEASON, A NEW CHANGE

DAY 12

Dear Diary,   *December 28, 2022*

Gerald came back home to my place. Exactly how God showed me would. Gerald had all of his clothes with him also. Almost as if he was ready to move back at that moment. That was not the case though, but I was still happy. Happy because God is real and God is faithful.

I told myself, this time, I will not mess anything up between Gerald and I. Not my will be done, but God's will be done.

I was hoping Gerald would tell me he would enter New Year's Eve with me, but going to church to watch the night service, but Gerald was still going to a strip club with his cousin in New York. I smiled and told Gerald that he deserves to have fun and do what makes him happy. I could tell that made Gerald feel great inside because he hugged me instantly after saying that.

I also did not check Gerald's phone.

God told me, for the next couple of days, to be Gerald's peace, even if you do not agree with Gerald's actions.

Ladies, sometimes, the man this is meant for you, will be the opposite of prince charming. It may be the man who is an alcoholic, a gambler, a liar, or even a cheat, who God had designed for you to be with. Do not take this as settling for less, but to understand God has the power to change these types of men through your prayers and as God changes them he changes you. Let God change them.

Our biggest problem in relationships is we think we can change people.

We cannot change anyone. Even if you think you are cracking away at changing a person, you will be fooled.

You cannot change what is already planted in a tree or flower. So how can you think about changing what is already planted in someone?

Maybe you could water and feed a plant or tree to grow, but just because it grows does not mean it will change its nature.

It's through different seasons of weather, fall, spring, summer, winter, that we see the change in plants, through their colors.

Sometimes in these seasons, such as fall, the color varies. The leaves on the tree may be brown, yellow, orange, or stay green throughout every season. Understand we as people are the same way. We either change bright in colors, dark in colors, or remain the same color each season; ultimately never changing at all.

Allow God to change people within, through every season they face.

As my mother always taught me, if the change never happens in the individual you are praying and hoping for, that means the change has already started to begin in you.

God's process may sound odd, like telling you to hold on to man like Gerald, but that is the beauty in how God works!

Obedience is better than sacrifice.

So, I cooked Gerald a great meal, gave him a back rub while he sat in between my legs enjoying his food.

Gerald and I cuddled after dinner and watched movies. We enjoyed each other's company. I could tell we were in a new and better space. The vibes were positive between us. There was nothing but laughter and peace.

I prayed before we went to sleep, that God would allow us to keep the peace, and God did.

Sincerely,
Happy

Chapter 13

OBEDIENCE LEADS TO
GOD'S PROMISE

DAY 15

Dear Diary,   *December 31, 2022*

I am aware that I skipped day thirteen and day fifteen. Those days were skipped because I was dwelling in peace and happiness. Which was something I did not have in a while.

Gerald and I enjoyed each other's company, like old times, but this time it was better. However, I still had no response from Gerald on if Gerald would be going to church with me on New Year's Eve. I chose not to mention it, although it pondered in my mind, nonstop. I just had to be obedient to God.

Gerald's cousin had called him stating that he would pick Gerald up later on New Year night. I honestly was not upset anymore. Although, if Gerald were to go with his cousin in New York for New Year's Eve, that would be the opposite vision God showed me.

If Gerald was the promise God had me wait for, then it was crucial that Gerald and I walked into the New Year together.

Instead of mentioning anything about New Year's Eve, I spent today braiding my hair, doing my makeup, and I went to the mall to buy a cute outfit.

When I arrived back home from going to the mall, I asked Gerald, while he sat in my living room, would he have liked for me to drop him off at his cousin's house for the New York party. Gerald told me no because he had already told his cousin the other day that he was not going to go. Gerald said his preference was to start his New Year's off with God and me.

Trust God's process, even when things are not going the way God showed you. I did not have to say anything to Gerald to change his mind. When you let God be fully in control, God will fight your battles for you.

When Gerald and I went to church tonight, Gerald was fully tuned in, to what our pastor was preaching about. I could tell he was truly receiving the word in his heart and spirit. Gerald did however, mention that he had wished he was drunk tonight. I tried to ignore him, but I could tell as happy as he was to be with me in church. A big part of him had wished he was in New York. Knowing Gerald felt this way, made me feel incomplete.

I remember after service, walking back into the house, feeling discouraged.

Gerald and I just said happy New Year's and took many pictures smiling, but I do not feel as happy as I looked in our pictures.

I asked God, "Why do I feel like this? Why do I feel like I still have not received my promise, if Gerald returned like you said he would?" God responded, "It is because Gerald was never your promise, Gerald was just attached to your promise."

Listen if God tells you what your promise is, always know that, you will go through a journey to get to it. Even if you feel like you have finally reached the destination to your promise, there's still more traveling to do. This is where I was at in the process of walking to my promise. I reached the town in which my promise resided, but I still had more miles to go, to get to the address my promise resides at.

God said, "It was through your battle of what you went through with Gerald, that I was navigating you to your promise."

I thought this was a healing diary, because of how broken I was when Gerald and I had split. I never intended to turn my diary into a book. However, this book you are reading is my promise!

I hope that my journey can help all readers to navigate into a new prayer life with God. Moreover, I hope this book can help all readers get closer to where their promise lies and to walk into who God has called you all to be.

I would have never seen myself becoming an intercessor, evangelist, or an author. However, God changed my walk, my hands, my feet, my mind, my heart and my lenses when I allowed him to change me, when I thought I was completely torn apart. I am no longer the same. God made me a new creature in his image.

Some of you may say, "My story is different from your story." Which is fine.

Maybe you are not experiencing relationship issues. Maybe some of you are experiencing health issues or suffering from a dysfunctional family. Maybe some of you are battling an addiction that has a stronghold on you. Regardless of the battles all of you are facing, put it in God's hands. Allow God to fix your situation and fix you in the process.

Every battle we face in our lives, are designed to birth greatness!

Your battles will lead you to what God has stored up for you, in your treasure box, also referred to as, your promise.

Remove your plan and ask God about his plans for your life. Be obedient to God's plan and watch what the enemy thought would destroy you, become the greatest testimony of your life.

Also learn to work in the kingdom, for whatever it is that you are asking God for. We as Christians, assume God is supposed to give us what we ask for because the bible tells us in John 16 verse 24, *Ask, using my name, and you shall receive, and you will have abundant joy.*

How is it that we work hard at our jobs to pay for the things we want, but we do not want to work hard in our prayers, with our worship, with serving in God's house? You cannot expect much, when you are not doing much.

We all want so much from God, but fail to put the work in. The word of God tells us in Luke 12 verse 48, *When someone has been given much, much will be required in return*; and that is most certainly a life principle.

God is so amazing to us, that he will always bless us anyway, since we all fall short. We just have to aim to please God more, since God aims to love and care for us.

I never thought that my breakup from Gerald would transform me into the Godly woman I am today.

In the beginning of Gerald and I's split, I was broken, tired, depressed and frustrated. I honestly felt as if God was almost punishing me for my past mistakes.

For the strong readers that are reading this, you are probably saying, "Ebony get over it. It is life. Move on." If you feel this way, just wait until you fall in love with someone and I mean real love, and they break your heart. You will understand why there's a phrase that says, *Love is the worst drug*.

I looked at my break up with Gerald as the devil trying to destroy Gerald and I, like the enemy does to people who are intoxicated. Not realizing that I gave the devil too much power over my situation.

I was wondering why am I still going through this with Gerald for so long, if I always put God first. The reality was I was defeating my own prayers, when I acknowledged and gave the devil power, instead of acknowledging that God caused this storm. God caused this storm, so that God could speak to me, in a way he has not spoken to me before. Or God was speaking to me this way before, but I was not listening.

This storm in my life was God raising his voice louder, so I can hear him fully. Moments like these, we get mad at God, when God is simply discipling us. Just think about it. If your parents or guardians never disciplined you as a child, you would have never learned from your mistakes. Instead trouble will always follow you.

The world will damage you worse than your parents' discipline. This is why when most of us become adults, we thank our parents for their discipline. It is understood, in adulthood, that disciplining is necessary and it is an act of love.

God is the exact same way.

Have you ever stopped to realize that maybe that job you lost, that health battle, or your past traumas was an act of discipline from God and not an attack from God or the enemy?

The enemy will only attack what we let him.

The scripture tells us in James 4 verse 7, So humble yourselves before God. Resist the devil, and he will flee from you.

If you speak and acknowledge the enemy, by saying the simplest things like, "The devil has thought he won or I have been attacked on every side by the devil, but I rebuke him", you are sadly still acknowledging the enemy. You are not allowing him to fully flee from you.

There is power in what you say! So much so that the bible says in Proverbs 18 verse 21, *The tongue can bring death or life; those who love to talk will reap the consequences.*

Be mindful of what you say and how you say it.

Remember our scripture also tells us in James 1 verse 19, *Understand that, my dear brothers and sisters: You must all be quick to listen, slow to speak, and slow to get angry.*

We are failing to listen to what God is saying to us about our situations, so that we can know what to say when we pray to him.

Oftentimes we wonder if God is really listening to our prayers, because if he is, why are we still suffering? Why are we still struggling? Why are we still battling sickness, financial stress and still unhappy? If God is real, why are we stuck in difficult situations, even when we give God our all? Honestly, these are questions we should stop asking God about so much and ask ourselves.

Our anger blocks us from listening and understanding God's will.

God is always speaking to us, it is just, we are not fully listening.

I am going to drop a gem to you all, on why it is so difficult to hear God when you are facing trials and tribulations. It is because we complain entirely too much.

You want to make God upset? Then go complain.

You are making yourself wait longer to come out of your depression, your struggles and your hardships, when you complain.

I know that the old church mothers would always tell us, "Baby, talk to God about all of your troubles and he will fix it." The reality is, God knows all of our troubles before you talk to him about. So when you talk to God about your troubles, do not mention how you are tired. Do not mention how you are frustrated. Do not mention how you are ready to throw in the tile. Change your pain into praise. Tell God, "I may not understand, but I trust you. God, heal my hurt. God, take away my anger. God, give me peace that surpasses my understanding. God, strengthen me when I feel weak. This can be much easier said than done, but nothing in life is ever meant to be easy, especially your walk with God. It can be hard just to wake up and pray because sometimes we have many problems consumed in our minds, but God always loves a challenge. You set yourself up for blessings from God, when you push past your challenges. We may not always see the rewards from God in physical form, but know that your rewards are definitely present.

Some rewards may be that God healed your loved ones who were sickly. Other rewards may be that God gave you a roof over your head. Moreover, a reward could be that God blessed you with a new job opportunity. Lastly, a reward God gave you was that he allowed you to still keep your car and not have it repossessed after missing three car payments.

Other rewards from God may be for your friends, family or your future generation of children. The great thing about this is, your friends, family or future generation of grandchildren may or may not go on a different religious path than you, maybe becoming Buddhist. Nevertheless they will still be covered by the blood of Jesus because of God's mercy, grace, love and favor towards us.

Your friends, family, or future grandchildren will have everything they need because of the work you put in, through your worship, praise, faithfulness and obedience. God will always honor your work towards him and bless your generations of family.

That is one of the greatest rewards that God can give us because some of your family's disobedience could have led them to a dangerous path, but God's grace, mercy, love and favor helped to turn it around.

Some of your families may have been headed towards death, but the work you put in God's kingdom, helped to save them!

Everything we do for God, serves a divine purpose. A purpose bigger than our understanding.

This information I gave you all, helped me to not only receive what I wanted from God, but helped me to understand why it was necessary for me to go through difficult trials.

Moreover, I learned that God will never give a promise to you in its full entirety. There will always be more attached to your promise, that will come with multiple assignments. It will never be a one and done situation.

Here I was, thinking to myself, "Ok God, you promised me that I would become successful. God, you promised me that I would become a millionaire. God, you promised me that Gerald and I would be happily married." Just for me to understand the promise God was referring to was not any of these things, although my promise had these blessings connected to it.

God revealed to me that my promise was to become an author and to minister the word of God, which is the opposite of anything I wanted to do.

God showed me, me preaching and teaching his word.

I tried to go to school for business and it did not work. I tried to start my own clothing line and it did not work. I tried to become a model at Barbizon modeling agency and it did not work. I tried to become a hairstylist based on my high clientele and it still did not work. I tried to become a makeup artist and it did not work. So many talents, so many gifts, but if it is not in God's agenda, it will not work, regardless of how long I tried.

The best part of God's promises is that, even if you have not learned how to hear from God, he will always send messages to grab your attention. God will send his message as many times as he needs to.

Before I started listening to God, many prophets told me "Ebony, go write the book", but I did not listen. Family members would tell me how strong and admirable I was, encouraging me to tell my story in a book, but I still did not listen.

I will never forget being twelve years old, attending church each and every Sunday with my mom.

One particular Sunday, the church had a world-renowned prophet come visit to speak a word to God's people. This prophet was so big that other churches would all come together when they knew he was coming to town. Everyone gets excited because they want to hear their word from the Lord and this man was the real deal!

So, I remember me also being excited for this service, because prophets also speak words over children's life.

During the service the prophet entered, giving people prophecies before he touched the mic. He had not said anything to me, but when he did speak on the mic, he prophesied to another family and suddenly I caught the spirit, rejoicing for another family's word from God. It was my first experience catching the holy ghost. I started jumping up and down, leaping and yelling out, "Hallelujah". I was crying and speaking in a heavenly language.

After I finished rejoicing, the prophet gave a word to the person next to me, but still said nothing to me. As I looked around, you could tell everyone was hoping that they would receive a word from God. I guess because the prophet was telling individuals, "That house is about to be yours and God is about to pay your college tuition in full." The prophet even made a lady take out her breathing tubes and told her to walk around the building without it. Instantly she was healed! Literally miracles were being released during the entire service! However, the prophet still said nothing to me.

Once the service was over, everyone was conversating, putting on jackets and heading home. The prophet however, was still giving a few people words from God as they were leaving out.

I grew discouraged because as many times the prophet came near me and glanced over at me, he had no word from God for me. I saw other children, including my friends, rejoicing and receiving their words from God, but not me. It did feel amazing catching the holy spirit though. I felt refreshed. It is an unexplainable feeling everyone should encounter, but I still wanted the prophet to give me a word from the Lord.

As my mom and I headed out the door, the prophet stopped me and walked over to me. Not my mom, he asked for me. The prophet said, "Lift your hands. You are going to be incredibly blessed. God is going to make sure not only you are blessed but you have generational wealth. People are not going to understand why you are so blessed, but they will look up to your story. Many young women will admire your story. You are a leader. Be blessed in Jesus name."

Then he left.

In that moment, I learned that God will never count you out, especially when you praise God for others. To hear the prophet tell me that was exciting, but it made me afraid of what my future entailed, since he said people will admire my story.

It is now thirteen years later, and that message has more value than it did back then.

God's word has power. It does not matter if you are a different religion, non-religious or atheist. God will always deliver his message. You just make the choice of listening to it.

Sincerely,
Choosing God

Chapter 14

THE CHOICE TO WALK
INTO GOD'S PROMISE

DAY 16

Dear Diary, *January 1st, 2023*

Today was not great. Although Gerald came to church with me, it still was unpleasant. In fact, Gerald and I argued badly. I did not sit next to him during service.

After church service, Gerald and I went downstairs to reconcile our differences in a private area. Which was actually quite embarrassing. My mind kept questioning, "Is this what you prayed for? Is this what you fasted for? Is this really your promise?" Even if this was not my promise and Gerald is just attached to it, I still do not want it. You see how just that quick the enemy can make you feel like the journey to obtaining your promise was not worth it.

As my mind wondered, I knew that I could not turn back and I had to work out my differences with Gerald. So Gerald and I went into a private area and discussed what made us both upset.

Gerald and I fortunately did mediate our differences. We both agreed we came too far, just to give up! God will always get the glory!

After things were better between us, we went back to my home and I cooked dinner for Gerald. My family came over as well. We all watched movies, conversated, played games, and had a great time.

Once my family left and went home, Gerald told me to go to bed while he cleaned up the house, put away the leftover food and took the trash out. Gerald knows these are qualities that I love, because most men hate to clean up.

When Gerald had finished, he came to lay in bed with me. He began to express to me how much he loves me and how our relationship means the world to him. The argument we had earlier today had no meaning to him.

I knew in my heart the love Gerald and I share is real, we just have to work harder towards growing.

Suddenly, it hit me! Yes, for these past days and weeks I prayed for my relationship, but God wanted to reveal to me that he was giving me power! I have the power to control how my relationship is. I have the power to control my health and my career. It is not my power, it is God's power and with God's power you can overcome and achieve anything!

Many of us may question and say, "Well, if that's true, why am I not wealthy yet?"

I know it can seem as if most of the people in this world, who are non-believers, are the wealthy ones, but the only power they have is money. Well, actually, it is reversed. Money has power over them. Money has so much power over them that it has caused, slavery, sex-trafficking, drug smuggling, gamblers, sweatshops and more. All these examples are people who gain money to control others because the money is controlling them.

Have you ever stopped to think, maybe God did not allow you to become successful yet because he did not want the money to control you?

God knows the damage it costs being controlled by money and how it ruins our lives in the end. We hear so many stories of how money will change people and how money will show people's true colors. People will even mention how the scripture states in 1 Timothy 6 verse 10, For the love of money is the root of all kinds of evil. And some people, craving money, have wandered from the true faith and pierced themselves with many sorrows.

This scripture can be contradicting because if it is the root to all evil, why is it everyone on this planet wants wealth? I am going to answer this question for you who are curious about this scripture. Money is the root of evil, if you let it.

Remember everything in this life is a choice. Your faith, your partner, your job, it is all a choice. Even doctors will give you the choice after giving birth to either keep your child or give your child up for adoption. Some of us even have the option to even abort the baby, in the beginning stages of pregnancy. If you choose God's power over your life decisions, your money will never be rooted to evil and your money will not control you.

Once I grabbed this in the spirit before going to sleep with Gerald, God identified to me that it was through his power that I would be able to control the things in my life. How is that? It is through my prayers. Not only do my prayers have power, but they give me Godly power in return.

Use this Godly power to take back the things that the devil thought he stole from you. Use your Godly power to get what you want from God. Get up and get your children back! Go get your relationship back! Go get your business back! Go get your health back! Go get your joy back!

When you go get your blessings, make sure to pray and ask God if this aligns with his will. Ask God to reveal it to you. If this does not align with God's will, ask God, what is his will for your life?

Remember if God placed anything in your heart, then it is attached to your promise! You are meant to have what your heart desires. If you do not have everything your heart desires yet, it is because most likely, God is making you wait for a divine purpose. A purpose that is bigger than you or your understanding.

Trust God's will. It will all eventually make sense, at God's perfect timing. When it is your time, after walking with God, you will walk into your promise!

Sincerely,
Walking into my promise

Bibliography

NLT and ERV BY Tyndale House Publishers Inc. Holy Bible, New Living Translation, Easy-To-Read Version copyright 1996, 2004, 2007, 2015 by Tyndale House Foundation.

- 2 Peter 1:3-5
- 2 Peter 3:9
- John 10:10
- Judges 13
- Numbers 23:19
- Isaiah 40:31
- 2 Timothy 1:7
- Psalms 23:5
- Nehemiah 8:10
- Psalms 34:7
- Deuteronomy 31:8
- Psalms 100:4
- Lamentations 3:23
- John 16:24
- Luke 12:48
- Proverbs 18:21
- James 1:19
- James 4:7
- 1 Timothy 6:10
- Proverbs 25:15
- Luke 18:1